ROMANO GUARDINI

MODERN SPIRITUAL MASTERS

Robert Ellsberg, Series Editor

This series introduces the writing and vision of some of the great spiritual masters of the twentieth century. Along with selections from their writings, each volume includes a comprehensive introduction, presenting the author's life and writings in context and drawing attention to points of special relevance to contemporary spirituality.

Some of these authors found a wide audience in their lifetimes. In other cases recognition has come long after their deaths. Some are rooted in long-established traditions of spirituality. Others charted new, untested paths. In each case, however, the authors in this series have engaged in a spiritual journey shaped by the influences and concerns of our age. Such concerns include the challenges of modern science, religious pluralism, secularism, and the quest for social justice.

At the dawn of a new millennium this series commends these modern spiritual masters, along with the saints and witnesses of previous centuries, as guides and companions to a new generation of seekers.

Already published:

Dietrich Bonhoeffer (edited by Robert Coles)
Simone Weil (edited by Eric O. Springsted)
Henri Nouwen (edited by Robert A. Jonas)
Pierre Teilhard de Chardin (edited by Ursula King)
Anthony de Mello (edited by William Dych, S.J.)
Charles de Foucauld (edited by Robert Ellsberg)
Oscar Romero (by Marie Dennis, Rennie Golden, and Scott Wright)
Eberhard Arnold (edited by Johann Christoph Arnold)
Thomas Merton (edited by Christine M. Bochen)
Thich Nhat Hanh (edited by Robert Ellsberg)
Rufus Jones (edited by Kerry Walters)
Mother Teresa (edited by Jean Maalouf)
Edith Stein (edited by John Sullivan, O.C.D.)
John Main (edited by Laurence Freeman)
Mohandas Gandhi (edited by John Dear)
Mother Maria Skobtsova (introduction by Jim Forest)
Evelyn Underhill (edited by Emilie Griffin)
St. Thérèse of Lisieux (edited by Mary Frohlich)
Flannery O'Connor (edited by Robert Ellsberg)
Clarence Jordan (edited by Joyce Hollyday)
Alfred Delp, SJ (introduction by Thomas Merton)
Karl Rahner (edited by Philip Endean)
Sadhu Sundar Singh (edited by Charles E. Moore)

MODERN SPIRITUAL MASTERS SERIES

ROMANO GUARDINI

Spiritual Writings

Selected and Translated with an Introduction by

ROBERT A. KRIEG

ORBIS BOOKS
Maryknoll, New York 10545

Founded in 1970, Orbis Books endeavors to publish works that enlighten the mind, nourish the spirit, and challenge the conscience. The publishing arm of the Maryknoll Fathers and Brothers, Orbis seeks to explore the global dimensions of the Christian faith and mission, to invite dialogue with diverse cultures and religious traditions, and to serve the cause of reconciliation and peace. The books published reflect the views of their authors and do not represent the official position of the Maryknoll Society. To learn more about Maryknoll and Orbis Books, please visit our website at www.maryknoll.org.

Published by Orbis Books, Maryknoll, NY 10545-0308.

Grateful acknowledgment is made to Matthias Grünewald Verlag (Mainz, Germany) for permission to translate the copyrighted material contained in this book.

Manufactured in the United States of America

Library of Congress Cataloging-in-Publication Data

Guardini, Romano, 1885-1968.
[Selections. English. 2005]
Romano Guardini : spiritual writings / selected and translated with an introduction by Robert A. Krieg.
p. cm. – (Modern spiritual masters)
ISBN 1-57075-589-2 (pbk.)
1. Spiritual life – Catholic Church. I. Krieg, Robert Anthony, 1946- II. Title. III. Modern spiritual masters series.
BX2350.3.G83 2005
248.4′82 – dc22

2004026570

Contents

Preface

The Gotthard Chapel, adjoining the cathedral of Mainz, Germany, is a point of stillness. Small and dimly lit, this medieval space focuses one's attention on a simple altar and a wooden crucifix. At the same time, because of the way the chapel is situated, it permits those at prayer to hear faintly both the hymns being sung in the cathedral and also the voices of shoppers outside on the central plaza of Mainz. The Gotthard Chapel is one of the places in which Romano Guardini prayed during his youth. Today, as in the late 1800s, it nurtures the contemplative spirit found in the numerous writings of Guardini. To read Guardini's books and essays is to enter into a quiet chapel where the sacred and the secular come together in the mystery of Christ.

This book is a guide into Romano Guardini's reflections on Christian faith and contemporary life. It contains selections from the theologian's spiritual and theological writings; it does not include his work on such topics as world literature, Western society, or modernity. This anthology organizes Guardini's texts around five religious themes: human life in God's presence, the mystery of God, Christian belief, the living Christ, and types of prayer. The book's structure would probably trouble Guardini because he deliberately avoided putting his ideas into a grand theological system. Yet, similar to Guardini's approach, the chapters locate his thought in relation to his experience and his prayer. Each chapter begins with Guardini's memoirs, then moves through his reflective writings in chronological order, and concludes with a prayer by Guardini. The biblical verse at the start of each chapter comes from one of the psalms discussed by Guardini in his book *The Wisdom of the Psalms.*

Romano Guardini wrote all of his published texts in German. This anthology brings some of Guardini's texts from German into English for the first time. It also provides fresh translations of texts that appeared in English from the 1930s into the 1960s. I chose to translate anew all of the texts that are included here in order to employ key terms consistently and to use contemporary idioms.

This Guardini reader complements Heinz R. Kuehn's *The Essential Guardini: An Anthology of the Writings of Romano Guardini* (Chicago: Liturgy Training Publications, 1997), which is, to my knowledge, the only collection of Guardini's texts in English to show thc breadth as well as the depth of the theologian's work. Heinz Kuehn has brought to his anthology the direct, personal knowledge of Romano Guardini that he and his wife, Regina Kuehn, reached during their years with the priest-professor in Berlin. My selection of texts has been influenced in part by *The Essential Guardini* and also in part by Ingeborg Klimmer's *Angefochtene Zuversicht: Romano Guardini Lesebuch* (Mainz: Matthias Grünewald, 1985), which gives a representative selection of Guardini's theological writings.

Although I never saw or heard Romano Guardini, I have come to regard him as a sage and a mentor. Each time that I read or reread a text by him, I am enlightened about God, human life, and Christian belief, and I am inspired to move toward my own center of stillness. Guardini's texts speak to the heart as well as to the mind as they invite contemplation and new questions. I wish to thank Robert Ellsberg, editor-in-chief of Orbis Books, for initiating this anthology and guiding it to completion.

The Christian faith is primarily known through the witness of Jesus' followers. I am grateful to Richard F. Kyle, C.S.C., Patrick J. Lynch, C.S.C., and Herman F. Zaccarelli, C.S.C., for living the truths about which Romano Guardini wrote.

I dedicate this book to my wife, soul mate, and color coordinator, Elizabeth.

ROBERT A. KRIEG

Chronology

1885	Born on February 17, in Verona, Italy. Moves with his parents to Mainz, Germany.
1903–10	University studies in Tübingen, Munich, Berlin, Freiburg, and Mainz.
1910–12	Ordained a priest and enters into pastoral ministry.
1912–15	Studies at Freiburg lead to a doctorate in theology.
1915–20	Resumes full-time pastoral ministry. Writes *The Spirit of the Liturgy* (1918).
1920–22	Studies at Bonn lead to his "Habilitation" (second doctorate) in theology.
1923–39	Professor at the University of Berlin and chaplain to Quickborn at Burg Rothenfels. Writes *The Church and the Catholic* (1923), *The Conversion of St. Augustine* (1935), and *The Lord* (1937).
1939–45	Dismissed from his professorship; "retires" in Berlin and then Mooshausen. Writes *The World and the Person* (1939) and *The Rosary of Our Lady* (1940).
1945–47	Professor at the University of Tübingen.
1948–63	Professor at the University of Munich. Preaches at St. Ludwig's Church. Named a papal prelate by Pope Pius XII in 1952. Writes *The End of the Modern World* (1950) and *Rilke's Duino Elegies* (1953).

1963–68 Retires from the University of Munich; his academic chair is given to Karl Rahner. Writes *The Virtues* (1963) and *The Wisdom of the Psalms* (1963). In 1965, declines Pope Paul VI's invitation to become a cardinal.

1968 Dies on October 1. Leaves a literary corpus of more than sixty books and a hundred essays.

Sources and Acknowledgments

The selections in this book were translated from their original German texts into English by Robert A. Krieg. In the bibliographic information below, the names of two publishers have been abbreviated: "MGV" means Matthias Grünewald Verlag (Publisher), and "WV" refers to Werkbund Verlag (Publisher). Each German text's date of first publication is given in this book's five chapters, while the date of a more recent edition of the German text usually appears below. The title and date of Guardini's books in English are given below after the information about the original German texts. The bibliographic citations in this book's introduction and chapters refer to the German texts. When a German text has been published in English, its bibliographic citation specifies the chapter as well as the pagination of the German edition; this information is added so that readers can more easily find the text in the English edition of the respective book.

AS *Die Annahme seiner selbst* (Mainz: MGV, 1987).

BML *Berichte über mein Leben* (Düsseldorf: Patmos Verlag, 1984).

CI "Christliche Innerlichkeit," in *Wille und Wahrheit* (Mainz: MGV, 1950).

EAN "Die Entfernung des Andromeda-Nebels," in *In Spiegel und Gleichnis* (Mainz: MGV, 1990).

EC *Die Existenz des Christen* (Paderborn: Schöningh Verlag, 1977).

EN	*Das Ende der Neuzeit* (Mainz: MGV, 1989). *The End of the Modern World* (1956).
GRC	"Ein Gespräch vom Reich Christi," in *Wurzeln eines grossen Lebenswerk,* vol. 1, ed. Franz Henrich (Mainz: MGV, 2000).
HE	*Der Herr* (Mainz: MGV, 1997). *The Lord* (1954).
HG	"Das Hindurchgehen," in *Geistliche Schriftauslegung* (Mainz: MGV, 1980). *Jesus Christ* (1959).
JB	*Johanneische Botschaft* (Freiburg: Herder Verlag, 1962).
LLB	*Liturgie und liturgische Bildung* (Würzburg: WV, 1966).
MA	*Die Macht* (Mainz: MGV, 1989). *Power and Responsibility* (1961).
MEN	*Den Menschen erkennt nur, wer von Gott weiss* (Mainz: MGV, 1987).
MST	"Der neue Mensch in der Sicht des Theologen," in *Im Brennpunkt—Der neue Mensch,* ed. Gunthar Lehner (Munich: Lucas Cranach Verlag, 1961).
RLF	*Der Rosenkranz Unserer Lieben Frau* (Würzburg: WV, 1949). *The Rosary* (1955).
RM	*Der Raum der Meditation* (Mainz: MGV, 1980).
TAO	"Tagebuch: Aus Oberitalien," in *In Spiegel und Gleichnis* (Mainz: MGV, 1990).
TBF	*Theologische Briefe an einen Freund* (Munich: Ferdinand Schöningh Verlag, 1976).

TG *Theologische Gebete* (Frankfurt am Main: Josef Knecht Verlag, 1948). *Prayers from Theology* (1959).

TU *Tugenden* (Würzburg: WV, 1963). *The Virtues* (1967).

VB *Vorschule des Betens* (Mainz: MGV, 1986). *Prayer in Practice* (1957); *The Art of Praying* (1994).

VG *Vom Geist der Liturgie* (Mainz: MGV, 1997). *The Spirit of the Liturgy* (1935).

VL *Vom Leben des Glaubens* (Mainz: MGV, 1935). *Life of Faith* (1961).

VLG *Vom lebendigen Gott* (Mainz: MGV, 1981).

VSK *Vom Sinn der Kirche* (Mainz: MGV, 1990). *The Church and the Catholic* (1935).

VZ *Von heiligen Zeichen* (Mainz: MGV, 1990). *Sacred Signs* (1956).

WC *Das Wesen des Christentums* (Mainz: MGV, 1991).

WP *Weisheit der Psalmen* (Mainz: MGV, 1987). *The Wisdom of the Psalms* (1968).

WU *Welt und Person* (Würzburg: WV, 1950). *The World and the Person* (1965).

ZKG "Zwei Kapitel zur Gotteslehre," *Die Schildgenossen* 15 (July 1936): 396–408.

•

Grateful acknowledgment is made to the Katholische Akademie in Bayern (Munich, Germany) for permission to reprint the photograph of Romano Guardini that appears on this book's cover. The Katholische Akademie holds the copyright to this photograph, which was taken in 1955 when Guardini was seventy years old. Also, grateful acknowledgment is given to Matthias Grünewald Verlag (Mainz, Germany) for permission to reprint from copyright material the texts contained in this book. Matthias Grünewald Verlag holds the rights to these writings by Romano Guardini.

Introduction

A Christian Humanist

Romano Guardini (1885–1968) was a man of letters, a priest, and a professor in Germany. He was also one of the most creative Catholic theologians between the First Vatican Council (1869–70) and the Second Vatican Council (1962–65), publishing over sixty books and one hundred essays.

Romano Guardini is comparable to John Henry Newman (d. 1890), whose writings Guardini read. Like Newman, Guardini thought outside the theological categories of his day, knew well the history of the church and its teachings, and saw the contemporary church's struggles and concerns in relation to a profound understanding of human life in God's presence. Like Newman, Guardini stood at odds with ecclesiastical officials who were suspicious of his theological writings and his pastoral leadership. Unlike Newman, Guardini did not become a cardinal. In 1879, Newman was invited into the college of cardinals by Pope Leo XIII and said yes. In 1965, Guardini was approached by Pope Paul VI but declined the pontiff's offer. In any case, like Newman, Guardini wrote books, essays, and prayers that contain a wealth of wisdom.

Guardini struggled with an issue that we still face, namely, how to speak about the truths of Christian belief. When we talk about God, Jesus Christ, and the Holy Spirit, we often seem to be discussing realities disconnected from our everyday lives. We can find ourselves using two unrelated vocabularies, one concerning our religious beliefs and the other concerning our social, economic, and political world. In short, we may experience a divided consciousness, a split between the sacred and the secular, the holy and the worldly. When we try to overcome this division by imposing religious categories on the secular arena, we end up misrepresenting or overlooking essential dimensions of reality. For example, when we primarily rely on religious words and ideas to describe our lives, we realize that we have ignored the insights afforded by psychology or by political and economic analysis. Yet when we employ secular language as well as talk about God, we are unsure of how the two realms of discourse relate to each other. What occurs on Sunday seems separated from what happens from Monday through Saturday. The split between our use of religious words and our reliance on secular words can bring about a polarization in ourselves and in the church. It seems that few people today can successfully use together God-talk and the ordinary discourse of modern life.

Romano Guardini sought to unite, or at least to make complementary, our talk about God and our talk about ourselves and our world. For over fifty years, he fashioned a language of Christian humanism, of Christian personalism, that allowed him to illumine both the mystery of God and the complexities of human beings. As the theologian Karl Rahner (d. 1984) observed in 1965, Guardini shed light on "the unspeakable mystery that we call God" and also on "the ultimately unspeakable qualities" of human beings. Guardini was convinced that as we gain a deeper understanding of God, we simultaneously arrive at a better knowledge of humanity. Conversely, as we attain valid insights into human life, we receive new glimpses of God. As Cardinal Joseph Ratzinger observed in 1996, Guardini placed Jesus Christ at the center of his thought. The twofold effort to know God and ourselves more fully occurs in a concentrated manner, Guardini maintained, when we reflect on the person and work of Jesus Christ, who is the full revelation of God and simultaneously the full revelation of human beings.

In order to attain his insights into the truths of Christian faith, Romano Guardini moved back and forth between divine revelation as known in the Bible and Christian tradition on the one hand, and modern life and contemporary issues on the other. On his seventieth birthday, he pointed out that Christian belief should bring about "a methodical encounter between faith and the world," in which "faith should speak and give answers" while "the world should pose questions to the faith and be illumined by that faith." Ten years later, Guardini noted that "on the basis of Christian faith, there should open a view of the world, a glimpse of its essence, an assessment of its values, that is otherwise not possible." At the same time, contemporary culture should enrich our Christian belief because "from the world and its problems questions are posed to revelation that bring this otherwise silent content to speech. In this ever new, changing encounter, there is attained a fruitful illumination of Christian existence."

Romano Guardini's dialogical approach to understanding the mysteries of God and of human life generated a unifying discourse about our lives from Sunday through Saturday. Guardini spoke of God as the ultimate personal reality, and he viewed men and women as potential persons in relation to God, self, and other human beings. As he developed this language of personalism, he kept returning to certain truths or themes at the heart of Christian belief. Among them were these five:

1. All men and women live to some degree and in some manner in relationship with God.

2. While God is one, God is also in some sense truly interpersonal or relational.

3. Christian belief involves one's whole self.

4. Jesus Christ remains alive and present to us through the Holy Spirit.

5. Prayer includes the unconscious yearning of our hearts for God.

These themes arose out of Guardini's own deepest stirrings and experiences. At the same time, his reflections directed him to enter more fully into the contemporary world, thereby turning his life into an unusual journey.

In Search of God and Self

Romano Guardini had a creative though lonely childhood. Born in Verona, Italy, on February 17, 1885, he moved during his first year with his parents to Mainz, Germany, where he grew up speaking Italian at home and German at school. During the week, Romano saw little of his father, who traveled extensively for his import-export business. He was close to his mother, having inherited her religious disposition and her tendency toward depression.

The young Romano excelled at school, learning Latin, Greek, French, and English. He became a voracious reader of writers like Dante, Shakespeare, and Rainer Maria Rilke. When he was not at school, Romano remained at home with his three younger brothers. An exception to his seclusion occurred during his last years in Mainz's Gymnasium (high school) for the Humanities when he participated in an informal reading group for exceptional students. This gathering of Catholic youth was initiated and led by the married couple Wilhelm and Josephine Schleussner, both of whom wrote books on Christian spirituality. The young Romano thrived in this intellectual circle, and eventually established similar reading groups for the remainder of his life.

During his university years, Guardini underwent a crisis of faith. He failed in his study of chemistry at the University of Tübingen during the 1903–4 academic year and subsequently did only moderately well in his study of economics at the University of Munich and the University of Berlin during 1904 and 1905. These negative experiences eroded Guardini's self-confidence and released "the flood waters of depression." At times, he was so despondent he considered suicide. He also questioned the truths of Christian belief and groped for a more mature understanding of the church's teachings. Through all of this, he was sustained by his reading of literature and by the cultural opportunities available in Munich and Berlin. Going to art museums, concerts, the theater, and movies, he developed a habit that he kept until his last years.

One afternoon in the summer of 1905, everything came to a head when Guardini and his friend Karl Neundörfer were discussing Christian belief and the church. In an event similar to the conversion of St. Augustine, Guardini received an insight into faith as self-involving assent to God and Jesus Christ as known in the church through the Holy Spirit. From this moment on, the fog that had covered Guardini for two years began to lift. Over the next few months, he received counseling from a "liberal" priest in Berlin and soon decided that he himself should become a priest. After studying theology at the University of Freiburg, the University of Tübingen, and Mainz's diocesan seminary, Guardini was ordained a priest on May 28, 1910. He would have been ordained six months earlier, but he was delayed by the bishop because he had questioned the authoritarian ways of the seminary's rector and staff, and because he had criticized neo-Scholasticism, about which more is said below.

From 1910 through 1922, Guardini combined pastoral ministry and the study of theology. Working in parishes in Mainz, he established reading groups of young men and women and led them in retreats. Through these activities, he joined in Germany's Catholic youth movement, which flourished after the First World War. In particular, he emerged as the spiritual leader of Quickborn, a national association of Catholic youth whose center was the medieval castle at Burg Rothenfels am Main, not far from Würzburg. This ministry engaged Guardini's love of learning and desire for God; he remained active in Quickborn even as he pursued further studies in theology. In 1915, he completed a doctorate in theology at the University of Freiburg, and, from 1920 to 1922, he studied at the University of Bonn and wrote his second doctoral dissertation, which was required for a professorship at a German university. Both of these dissertations treated aspects of the theology of St. Bonaventure and showed Guardini's affinity for the Neoplatonism that runs through the Gospel of St. John, the writings of St. Augustine and St. Bonaventure, and into the German idealism of such thinkers as F. W. J. Schelling. This intellectual orientation also led Guardini to the phenomenology of Max Scheler (d. 1928). In 1918 Guardini wrote *The Spirit of the Liturgy,* which uses Scheler's philosophical approach in describing and analyzing the essential elements and inner dynamics of Christian worship. This small book immediately won Scheler's praise and international recognition. It is still highly regarded by liturgical scholars.

Fashioning a Christian Humanism

In 1923, Guardini deliberately began to develop a Christian humanism. Drawing on the waters of divine revelation — available in Scripture and Christian tradition — Guardini attempted to quench the modern thirst for fresh answers to life's primary questions. As professor of "the philosophy of religion and the Catholic worldview" at the University of Berlin, he lectured on the New Testament and on the literature of St. Augustine, St. Anselm, Dante, Pascal, Hölderlin, Dostoyevski, and Rilke. These lectures attracted hundreds of listeners from the University of Berlin and from Berlin's cultural elite, and they generated essays and books on God, the New Testament, and the West's "great books." Guardini's listeners and readers marveled not only at his insights into human life and values, but also at his interdisciplinary approach to his topics, that is, at his use of history, phenomenology, literary criticism, and theology. While teaching in Berlin, Guardini presided and preached at Masses for the university's students, and he conducted retreats and seminars at Burg Rothenfels for the members of Quickborn. He eventually crafted his sermons, meditations, and reflections into such books as *The Living God, The Life of Faith,* and *The Lord.*

While Guardini's ideas and pastoral leadership were enthusiastically welcomed by the laity — Catholics and non-Catholics alike — they troubled church officials and theologians. This distrust arose in part because Guardini disregarded neo-Scholasticism, which was the only kind of philosophy and theology approved by the popes and the Vatican's Holy Office. Beginning in the mid-1800s, Pope Pius IX had supported the revival of the philosophical and theological ideas and methods of the Middles Ages, as these ideas and methods were presented by their "commentators" or interpreters in the 1600s. With the official backing of the papacy, neo-Scholasticism evolved into an ahistorical compilation of medieval philosophical and theological propositions that theologians used in a deductive manner of reasoning. Assuming that there were no new questions about human life, and hence no new answers, neo-Scholastic thought did not address the issues raised by modernity — such as the nature of the human psyche — nor did it incorporate new information and insights about human life — such as the results of medicine, psychology, and sociology. Introduced to neo-Scholasticism as a seminarian in Mainz, Guardini rejected it as "arid" and "intellectually stifling." He deliberately adopted contemporary forms of thought and relied on an inductive reasoning that made him attentive to contemporary experience and the issues that were foremost in people's lives. Because of this intellectual orientation, he lived and worked under a cloud of ecclesiastical suspicion for over forty years.

The bishops' distrust of Guardini was fueled, too, by his leadership of Quickborn. This national association of Catholic youth had no formal ties to a diocese or official Catholic structure. Hence, it remained outside the direct control of church authorities. Quickborn was founded as an organization governed by laity as well as clergy, and Guardini resisted the efforts of bishops to bring Quickborn under their ecclesiastical umbrella. He judged that Quickborn could serve the church better by remaining independent of ecclesiastical governance. He insisted that Quickborn would be fully Catholic, even though it would remain autonomous from the official church. This stance disposed some bishops to link Guardini with "liberalism" and "modernism."

Romano Guardini also came into conflict with the state. In 1939, he was dismissed by the Third Reich from his professorship because of his criticism of Hitler. He was banned from Burg Rothenfels and from public speaking in general. He withdrew from public life in order to avoid imprisonment. During his forced "retirement" in Berlin and then in Mooshausen, a village in the Allgäu Alps, Guardini devoted himself to writing books such as *The World and the Person, The Rosary of Our Lady, Prayer in Practice* (*The Art of Prayer*), and *The Death of Socrates*. He also drafted texts that he revised and published soon after the war: *Freedom, Grace and Destiny, Prayers from Theology, The End of the Modern World, Power and Responsibility,* and *Rilke's Duino Elegies*. Although the 1940s were difficult years for Guardini as he witnessed the horrors of the Third Reich, they were also a creative period for him.

After the war, Romano Guardini assumed an influential role in the forming of West Germany's democratic society with its racial, ethnic, cultural, and religious diversity. From 1945 to

1947, he was the professor of "the philosophy of religion and the Christian worldview" at the University of Tübingen, and, beginning in 1948, he was the professor of "the philosophy of religion and the Christian worldview" at the University of Munich. He was not, however, a member of either school's faculty of theology because church officials and theologians still did not regard his writings as a valid form of Catholic theology. Nonetheless, Pope Pius XII named Guardini a papal monsignor in 1952, an ecclesiastical honor that coincided with the secular honor of being named the recipient of the prestigious Peace Prize of the German Book Association. At the University of Munich, Guardini lectured on Christian ethics, and in public addresses and radio talks he spoke about the values needed to undergird a society intent on protecting human rights and respecting the dignity of every human being. For almost fifteen years, he preached every Sunday during the academic year at St. Ludwig's Church in Munich.

Horrified by Auschwitz, Guardini realized after the war that he himself had spread anti-Judaic ideas in some of his earlier writings. Henceforth, he eschewed the negative depictions of Jews and Judaism that he had included in *The Lord*. During the early 1950s, he urged Germans to support Chancellor Konrad Adenauer's legislation providing restitution to Holocaust survivors. Further, he promoted the sending of private contributions to Israel and took the initiative to invite Martin Buber to return to Germany. Representative of Guardini's religious concerns from the mid-1950s into the 1960s are his books *The Virtues* and *The Wisdom of the Psalms*.

In 1962, Guardini's health began to fail, and he was unable to give some of his lectures at the University of Munich. Nevertheless, he briefly traveled to Brussels, where he was honored by the European community for his advancing of humanism since the end of the First World War. In a formal ceremony, Prince Bernhard of the Netherlands presented Guardini with the

Erasmus Award, which recognizes "individuals or institutions who have made important contributions to European culture in respect to culture, the social sciences, or social questions."

Romano Guardini formally retired from the University of Munich in 1963. As his health degenerated, he appeared less and less in public and tried to resist the waves of depression that swept over him as he struggled with illness. Throughout the last years of his life, he wrote to his friend Pastor Josef Weiger at Mooshausen and told of his search for God and meaning amid his suffering. These letters, along with a prayer, were posthumously published in 1976 under the title *Theologische Briefe an einen Freund* (Theological Letters to a Friend). Eight years later, the autobiographical reflections that Guardini had written at Mooshausen from 1943 to 1945 appeared as the book *Berichte über mein Leben* (Reports on My Life). Romano Guardini died on October 1, 1968, and is buried in a chapel at St. Ludwig's Church.

The Human Heart and Divine Love

According to Romano Guardini, we can meet God this side of heaven and can even deepen our relationship with God during our earthly lives. Whereas St. Bonaventure spoke of the human mind moving toward God, Guardini explored how the human heart, that is, the core of one's being, can move toward greater intimacy with God. Indeed, according to Guardini, as we allow ourselves to turn to God and mature in our bonds with God, each of us becomes a human person, an "I" relating to God as the "you" or "other" in our lives. Essential to human life is the act of decentering ourselves in ourselves and acknowledging God as our life's center. When we surrender ourselves to God, we simultaneously develop as human persons in relationship with one another and with ourselves. Calling attention to the primacy of the human heart, Guardini wrote in *The Lord* (*Der Herr*):

> The important things in human life originate not in the mind alone, but in the heart and its love. Our love has its own reasons and aims to which we must surely be open, or we will understand nothing about our lives. If this is the case with us, what about God who is love? When the depth and power of God are involved, is not divine love capable of so much more than human love? God's love is so great that it must appear to be folly and irrational to anyone who does not live on the basis of love. (HE, pt. 1, ch. 3, p. 15)

A person's movement into greater union with God, however, need not occur. We are born, Guardini observed, with a divided heart, with a conflict at the core of our being. For the most part, we long for God. As St. Augustine said in his *Confessions,* "You have made us for yourself, O God, and our heart is restless until it rests in you." We sense in ourselves the paradox of which Jesus spoke: "Those who lose their life for my sake will find it" (Matt. 10:39). At the same time, we resist giving ourselves to God. We try to take an inordinate control of our lives; our egos want to determine the course of events and the actions of other people. In short, each of us wants to be a god while longing for the true God. In this perspective, history is the drama of men and women deciding whether to give their hearts over to God, or to turn in on themselves, thereby yielding to evil. Guardini observed:

> In the depths of the human heart — along with the yearning for one's eternal source from which comes every creature and in which alone is found the fullness of life — there lies the primal disposition of sin, the resistance against God, awaiting an opportunity to revolt. This

> deepseated anger rarely shows itself as such, as unveiled opposition to God. It usually remains disguised and acts against human beings who are bearers of God's holiness: against prophets, against apostles, against the saints, and against those devoted to God. Holy men and women do in fact irritate most of us. Something in us is annoyed by the life of someone who is holy. (HE, pt. 1, ch. 8, p. 50)

The persistent human longing for God comes about, said Guardini, because we are created in God's "image" (Gen. 1:26). The life and love that we bring to one another are a pale reflection of God, who is life and love. This truth was revealed to Moses when God told Moses the divine name: "I am who I am" (Exod. 3:14). God is the transcendent yet immanent personal reality; God is the interrelating of the Father, the Son, and the Holy Spirit. This divine communion is God's "heart," pure love. Moreover, although God is complete, God reaches out in love and creates what is not God, the "other," namely, creation. God is continually inviting all of creation to enter more fully into relationship with God. In particular, God intends for human beings to mature as human persons in relation with God. Guardini reflected on the significance of God in our lives when he wrote:

> What would it be like if God truly governed my life? I would know that God is real. Further, I would know God not by means of a complicated process of reasoning but on the basis of my ongoing encounters with God. I would know that God is the One who exists beyond all human ideas and names about God. I would know God as I can see the full flowering of a meadow, feel its freshness, and know what I mean if I choose to speak about it. I would know God as I can know other human beings as they are with their good qualities and with their shortcomings, with their goals, with their ways of acting, with their manner of being, with so many traits and abilities, springing

> from their spirit and making an impression on me. God would exist in me with the power of the divine being. God would be the origin, meaning, and goal of everything in my life. (HE, pt. 1, ch. 7, p. 43)

Faith is the surrendering of one's whole self to God, the giving over of one's heart to the "object" of our heart's primary desire, God. This abandoning of self brings about the discovery of one's true self. Here is the central paradox of human life. We die to ourselves when we acknowledge the true center of our lives, God, and this death leads us to new life. To be sure, faith includes truths about God, truths communicated in the Bible and in religious tradition. At the same time, faith is much more than a rational or "notional" assent. As Cardinal Newman observed, faith entails a "real" assent. It involves our whole selves, our hearts, as we acknowledge God as God, as the One who is the source of truth and life and love. Living out this acknowledgment, we become human persons, living heart-to-heart with God. Hence, Guardini wrote:

> We are called to share in the integrity of the One who possesses his power and sanctity in the pure freedom of love and is able therefore to exist above good and evil, above justice and injustice. God is the One in whom are realized the words, "Be perfect, therefore, as your heavenly Father is perfect" (Matt. 5:48). To live in this manner is not a matter of ethics because it would be impossible for us to live up to this command on our own power. Rather, to live in union with God is a matter of faith, of surrendering ourselves to a demand that is the fullness of grace. Such a life is not possible solely by means of human effort. (HE, pt. 2, ch. 1, p. 93)

Jesus Christ mediates the union between ourselves and God, the Father. Since he lived, died, and rose to new life in the right relationship with Abba, Christ has reconciled us with God and thus with our own hearts and with one another. As the Son of God, he revealed God's heart to us; he left no ambiguity about God's intention for creation and, in particular, for us. Jesus Christ was, as Guardini said, God's "envoy" to us, the revealer of God. At the same time, Jesus Christ disclosed the ambiguities of our hearts, and resolved these as he lived in steadfast faithfulness to God, even in the face of death and evil. Guardini said:

> Christ alone can guarantee us new life. We must eventually let go of everything but Christ. The clarity of our insights, the high quality of our actions, the purity of our intentions, the trustworthiness of our personal character, the validity of our personal or cultural history have their value, but they are only a preparation. We must eventually let go of everything. To become Christian means to rely only on Christ's word, abandoning ourselves to Christ and his guarantee of new life. (HE, pt. 2, ch. 12, p. 172)

✱ Prayer is our attending to God, our listening to the transcendent source of our lives. We pray as individuals, and we also pray as communities through worship and communal devotions. Beneath these conscious forms of acknowledging God, a persistent yearning exists in our hearts. This longing is itself prayer. As St. Paul declared, "we ourselves ... groan while we await for adoption, for the redemption of our bodies" (Rom. 8:23). The centrality of prayer in our lives was highlighted by Guardini when he observed: "We must persistently seek to penetrate the darkness so that it opens and releases light. We must always pray that God touches our hearts. In all that we do, we must somehow stay awake and look for a sign from the other side. This attentiveness is prayer 'without ceasing' (Acts 12:5) which surely finds itself heard" (HE, pt. 3, ch. 6, p. 220).

These five themes do not exhaust the wealth of Guardini's thought. They are complemented by his reflections on the Holy Spirit, evil, the church, culture, and literature, to name but a few other topics. All of these themes cluster around the two foci of Guardini's thought: the mystery of God and the complexity of human beings, the magnanimity of God's heart and the ambiguities of the human heart. Further, these themes are all contained in the mystery of the God-man, Jesus Christ.

Guardini's Intellectual and Political Context

Romano Guardini did not live in a desert, and he did not lecture and write based on direct communications from God. He resided in Mainz, Berlin, and Munich. As he himself pointed out, he wrote in response to the situations and the intellectual currents in which he found himself. For this reason, in order to understand Guardini's texts one must know something about their philosophical, political, and religious situation. Three aspects of this context will be mentioned here. Readers who are not immediately interested in phenomenology and German politics may wish to jump ahead five paragraphs to the section on the Second Vatican Council.

First, the intellectual or philosophical horizon within which Guardini worked was determined by the tension between neo-Kantianism and phenomenology. Beginning in the second half of the 1800s, philosophers at many German universities set out to overcome Idealism and to renew the philosophy of Immanuel Kant (d. 1804). Claiming that the thought of Hegel, Fichte, and Schelling was disconnected from and irrelevant to the knowledge actually being gained from the natural sciences and social sciences, especially psychology, they maintained that Kant's thought contained the resources by which to understand what is involved in human knowledge and to explain the relationship between human cognition and reality. Following Kant, neo-Kantians like Hermann Cohen, Paul Natorp, and Ernst Cassirer doubted that human beings can know things in themselves, and hence they did not pursue conventional metaphysics. Instead, they concentrated on the knowing subject, on human cognition, and they also took up what Kant had called "practical reason," which includes ethics. In the Kantian perspective, religious belief is ultimately about ethics, and Christian faith concerns Jesus as the exemplar of the ideal way of human life. Guided by this philosophical outlook, Adolf von Harnack presented Jesus of Nazareth solely as a moral teacher in his influential book *What Is Christianity?* (1900).

By the early 1900s, however, many German scholars were saying that neo-Kantian thought had fueled subjectivism in the German culture; that is, it had contributed to people losing touch with objective reality, with life's basic truths. As a remedy to this perceived overemphasis on the knowing subject, there emerged a new philosophical orientation called phenomenology, which was founded by Edmund Husserl (d. 1938) and enhanced by Max Scheler. While the philosophy of Kant and the neo-Kantians reflects on how we know, phenomenology focused on what we know. It calls for an attentiveness to and contemplation of all aspects of reality. Phenomenology relies on various forms of perception, especially intuition, as it seeks to describe the world's fundamental realities and underlying dynamics. Representative of this philosophical orientation are Rudolf Otto's *The Idea of the Holy* (1917) and Martin Heidegger's *Being and Time* (1927).

Guardini opted for phenomenology over neo-Kantianism. He judged that since all aspects of the world possess an objectivity, inquiring minds can know created realities in themselves. For this task, he turned to phenomenology. Moreover, he used this method within the horizon of Christian faith in order to illumine aspects of divine revelation. As mentioned earlier, Guardini's reliance on phenomenology is evident, for example, in *The Spirit of the Liturgy.* It is also manifest in *The Lord,* which is a sustained reflection on the living reality of Jesus Christ.

A second important element of Guardini's world was the drastic shifts in Germany's political system. The German empire (*Reich*), first under the rule of Kaiser Wilhelm I, came into existence in 1871 — fourteen years before the birth of Romano Guardini. It collapsed at the end of the First World War when Kaiser Wilhelm II abdicated the throne on November 8, 1918, the same year that *The Spirit of the Liturgy* appeared in print. Germans had their first experience of a parliamentary democracy beginning in January 1919 when they instituted the Weimar Republic. The Catholic Center Party played a crucial role in the Weimar government because it mediated among the various political parties. Among its goals, the Center Party pushed for German universities to include more Catholic students. As a result, the University of Berlin decided to offer courses in Catholic theology and appointed Romano Guardini in 1923 to assume responsibility for lecturing on Catholicism. After President Paul von Hindenburg selected Adolf Hitler to be Germany's chancellor on January 30, 1933, the German parliament voted on March 23, 1933, to suspend the Weimar Constitution and to recognize Hitler as the nation's dictator. The Third Reich came into official existence. Romano Guardini now found himself in a dictatorship, having already experienced a monarchy and a democracy. Twelve years later, Germany lay in ruins. Among the destruction in Berlin were Romano Guardini's possessions and the house that he regarded as his first and only real home. In 1949, the people of West Germany established the German Federal Republic and elected the Catholic statesman Konrad Adenauer as their nation's chancellor. Guardini threw his support behind this new democracy.

Romano Guardini was not disposed to politics in the strict sense. He was, however, aware of political issues since as a child he had heard his father speak forcefully in support of the separation between church and state in Italy. In his youth, he became attentive to the quality of Germany's political, social, and cultural life. As a young priest, he judged that the ethos of the Weimar Republic fostered an unhealthy individualism, and, in response, he introduced young Catholics to intense experiences of community when they gathered at Burg Rothenfels. Further, in *The Church and the Catholic* he presented the church as the mystical body of Christ, as the community in which we can meet Jesus Christ and deliberately live in union with Christ and in communion with one another. As a professor in Berlin, Guardini discerned that Hitler held a depersonalizing sway over the German people and that Nazi propaganda depicted the Führer as the savior of the German people. In response, Guardini wrote *The Lord* with its dominant theme that Jesus Christ is the one and only savior. Christ alone is the bearer of God's grace, God's *Heil.* In other words, *The Lord* conveyed an implicit political message: it is blasphemous to declare "Heil Hitler!" Woven into *The Lord* are political statements like this one: "God has authority over the nation's leader regardless of what this leader may influence, or want, or accomplish" (HE, pt. 5, ch. 2, p. 382). In 1945, as Guardini saw death and destruction throughout Germany, he thought about modernity's limitations, moral conundrums, and spiritual strengths and dangers. He eventually expressed his postwar reflections in *The End of the Modern World* and *Power and Responsibility,* which paint a dark picture of our times.

From Vatican I to Vatican II

A third factor shaping Guardini's thought was the tension in the church between two distinct perspectives on the church's teachings, structure, and mission. These two outlooks — to use the categories of the theologian Bernhard Lonergan (d. 1984) — are "classical consciousness" and "pluralistic consciousness." The former was dominant at the First Vatican Council and continues to be the outlook of some Catholics. The latter slowly gained credibility among Catholics during the 1900s, influenced the majority of bishops at the Second Vatican Council, and today remains strong among Catholics.

Classical consciousness rests on the conviction that there exists one set of ideal forms by which to express the truths of divine revelation, the truths about humankind, and the truths about the church's nature and purpose. This conviction deliberately dominated Catholicism from the mid-1800s to the mid-1900s. Pope Pius IX (1846–78) condemned modern ideas such as religious freedom and the separation between church and state in his "Syllabus of Errors" (1864) and convoked the First Vatican Council (1869–70) with the intention of having it confirm his teachings against modernity. The council did not achieve, however, everything for which the pontiff had hoped. It succeeded in condemning the use of new philosophies in theology in its Dogmatic Constitution on the Catholic Faith, *Dei Filius,* and in asserting papal infallibility in matters of faith and morals in its Constitution on the Church of Christ, *Pastor Aeternus.* It also implicitly reaffirmed the church's reliance on neo-Scholasticism. Pope Pius X (1903–14) energetically reinforced classical consciousness in Catholic thought by condemning "modernism" in 1907, instituting a network of spies who reported apparent breaches in "orthodoxy," and readily excommunicating — or at least removing from teaching positions — Catholics who adopted modern ideas. Among those who lost professorships was Guardini's revered teacher at Tübingen, Professor Wilhelm Koch (d. 1955). Pius X also condemned the Catholic journal *Hochland* because it published articles on books, arts, and plays that were created by non-Catholics. Pope Pius XI (1922–39) sustained this classical point of view by favoring nation-states governed by Catholic dictators, in particular, Mussolini in Italy, Franco in Spain, and Suarez in Portugal. In his encyclicals, Pius XI envisioned the emergence of a new Christendom that would eventually replace Europe's secular society. Pope Pius XII (1939–58) upheld the domination of classical consciousness in 1950 when he condemned new forms of theology in his encyclical *Humani Generis*.

Pluralistic consciousness springs from the conviction that truth can be expressed in various forms or modes appropriate to a particular culture or to a specific period in history. Whereas classical consciousness sees the unity of faith threatened by a diversity of forms, pluralistic or historical awareness insists that unity without diversity is reduced to a uniformity that stifles truth. Pope Leo XIII (1878–1903) implicitly supported this historical consciousness when he called for new studies into the thought of St. Thomas, for fresh approaches to the Bible, and for the church to adjust to the new social and economic conditions of the modern period. Pope Benedict XV (1914–22) refocused the church's mission when he sought to serve as a politically neutral mediator among the warring nations of the First World War. Moreover, he did not attempt to suppress the biblical, liturgical, and youth movements that were intent on recovering ancient ideas and modes of Christian life and worship. These movements contributed to the *nouvelle théologie* that blossomed in France during the 1940s, especially through the work of M. D. Chenu (d. 1990), Yves Congar (d. 1996), and Henri de Lubac (d. 1991). The *nouvelle théologie* highlighted both the permanent values and the historical and hence changing modes of Christian life, thought, and worship over the centuries. Pope Pius XII encouraged a pluralistic consciousness when in 1943 he urged biblical scholars to use new critical approaches to the Bible. He also expressed it when he acknowledged in his Christmas address of 1944 the merits as well as the risks of parliamentary democracy. (This address was the first positive public statement about democracy by a pope.) Finally, there were the efforts by Catholic scholars in the mid-twentieth century to bring about a new Christian humanism. Among the writings that give a fresh synthesis of the Christian tradition and modern thought were Jacques Maritain's *True Humanism* (1939), Henri de Lubac's *The Drama of Atheist Humanism* (1949), Pierre Teilhard de Chardin's *The Phenomenon of Man* (1955), Louis Bouyer's *Christian Humanism* (1959), and Thomas Merton's "Christian Humanism in the Nuclear Era" (1966).

The emergence of a pluralistic consciousness within Catholicism from the mid-1800s into the 1960s set the stage for the Second Vatican Council (1962–65). This constructive spirit showed itself when Pope John XXIII (1958–63) declared to the council that the church has nothing to fear from the modern world. Further, the pluralistic consciousness among the council's participants enabled them to initiate the renewal of Catholic worship in the Constitution on the Sacred Liturgy, to apply a variety of images and concepts to the church in the Dogmatic Constitution on the Church, to outline a Christian humanism in their Pastoral Constitution on the Church in the Modern World, and to acknowledge the principle of religious freedom in the Declaration on Religious Liberty.

A Precursor of Vatican II

Romano Guardini deliberately adopted a pluralistic consciousness during his studies as a seminarian in Freiburg and Tübingen, and he eventually manifested it in his activities and writings. He broke out of the conventional role of a parish priest as he devoted more and more time and energy to leading Quickborn and keeping it free from direct ecclesiastical control. He departed from neo-Scholasticism when he studied St. Bonaventure's writings on their own terms and interpreted them without relying on the methods and the language of neo-Scholasticism. At Burg Rothenfels, during the 1920s, Guardini disregarded church regulations when he pulled the altar away from the wall, turned it around, and faced the congregation as he presided at Mass. He also taught the congregation to respond aloud to the priest's prayers during Mass. He showed the same independence in his literary interpretations of biblical texts and in his use of literature in his theological reflections. Publishing his essays on non-Catholic literature in *Hochland,* he heightened ecclesiastical suspicion of his "modernist" tendencies. As already mentioned, Guardini rejected neo-Scholasticism, and brought together the Christian tradition and secular thought in a fresh theological synthesis concerning God and human life. Thus, he fashioned a Christian humanism that overcame the split between religious language and secular discourse.

Guardini was also unconventional in his discussions of standard theological topics. To be sure, he stood in continuity with the First Vatican Council as he emphasized the centrality of God's revelation in Christian faith and theology. But unlike Vatican I, he approached divine revelation not as a set of propositions about God, but as a personal encounter and an ongoing relationship between God and God's people. Similarly, Guardini wrote about Jesus Christ without explicitly mentioning the Christological doctrine of the Council of Chalcedon in AD 451 (i.e., that Jesus Christ is "truly God" and "truly man" in "one person"). Avoiding any suggestion that Christ is an idea or an abstract truth, he spoke of Jesus Christ as we would talk about any person, for example, by recounting his words, deeds, and sufferings as remembered in the Gospels. Further, Guardini reflected on the divine character of the church by considering it not as an institution but as a community. He framed Christian ethics in a new horizon when he avoided rules of conduct and spoke about the sacred dignity of the human conscience, the virtues, and Christian life as discipleship to Jesus Christ. In all of his activities and writings, Guardini demonstrated that the church could fruitfully adopt new forms of discourse and life, and hence that the church could assume a pluralistic consciousness while maintaining its orthodoxy.

Romano Guardini was surely a precursor of the Second Vatican Council. Given his successful adoption of a pluralistic awareness of Christian belief, he set the stage for the council's use of new forms of thought and language to discuss the church and its ways of relating to the world. The Decree on the Liturgy calls Catholics to see the Mass not as an occasion for private devotion, but as the worship of believers united in Christ. The Dogmatic Constitution on the Church clarifies that the church is a people of God and a sacrament before it is an institution. The Pastoral Constitution on the Church in the Modern World sets aside the neo-Scholastic view of the church as God's kingdom on earth and presents the church as an agent for the coming of God's kingdom among all peoples. The Decree on Religious Freedom acknowledges the sacred status of the conscience of every human being and the right of each man and woman to worship God as each chooses. These documents and other conciliar documents affirm and develop ideas that Guardini himself had promoted since the early 1900s. This similarity of thought is not surprising given the fact that Guardini's writings had influenced Pope Paul VI and many of Vatican II's bishops and their theological advisors; among whom were Cardinal Joseph Frings, Cardinal Joseph Höffner, Cardinal Franz König, Karl Rahner, Joseph Ratzinger, and likely Karol Wojtyla, the future Pope John Paul II.

Curiously, Guardini himself had mixed feelings about Vatican II's documents and their postconciliar implementation. In an address at Mainz in 1964 he warned liturgists that the recent changes in the Mass were often superficial and not guided by an adequate understanding of liturgical principles. In *The Church of the Lord* (1965) he expressed his concern that the Dogmatic Constitution on the Church did not sufficiently stress that the church is the rock or fortress protecting God's revelation in the world. Guardini's uneasiness about Vatican II and its implementation may have resulted from his age: he was eighty years old when the council ended. Also, it may be that Guardini was continuing to do what he had done since his youth, namely, to question what others took for granted and to think outside of the accepted categories. Further, Guardini's uneasiness about the council may have come about because of the waves of depression that afflicted him during his last years. In any case, Guardini was reluctant to participate in the new era that the Second Vatican Council inaugurated. Like Moses, he had led a faithful people to a new land, but he himself was unable to enter it.

How to Read Guardini's Writings

For over fifty years, Romano Guardini carefully crafted each of his numerous essays and books as he brought to light truths of Christian faith and human life. He wrote with such clarity and originality that he influenced, according to many philologists, the linguistic character of German literature. Like a diamond cutter, Guardini set out to free the truth of each topic that he picked up. As a result, some of his writings are exquisite jewels that still catch our attention and stir our hearts. Books like *The Spirit of the Liturgy, The Lord,* and *The End of the Modern World* may even qualify as classics in Western literature, comparable to the great books — Augustine's *Confessions,* Dante's *Divine Comedy,* and Rilke's *Duino Elegies* — that nurtured Guardini throughout his life. Some texts by Guardini convey a wisdom that speaks to people of every generation and culture.

Yet each of Guardini's books and essays originated in a specific context. Like a diamond fixed to a ring, each work had its original setting. If we want to view a text as Guardini intended it, we should see it in its context. Readers of Guardini's works will gain a more accurate understanding of their meaning if they read these books and essays with at least six guidelines in mind.

First, look for each text's central intention or underlying theme. For example, in *The End of the Modern World* Guardini set out to highlight modernity's merits and possibilities as well as its limits and dangers. He meant for the book to bring about a constructive engagement with modern society, not a reaction against it. Guardini himself modeled this orientation as he himself contributed to the building up of West Germany.

Second, recognize each text's genre and its significance for interpreting the text. For example, *The Lord* is not a historical reconstruction of Jesus' life and times. It is an inspirational work, a collection of meditations and sermons. While it contains historical information — some of which historians have revised since 1937 when the book appeared — it does not give an accurate chronology of Jesus' life, nor an accurate reconstruction of Jesus' Jewish world. Instead, it follows the story line of John's Gospel and describes Jesus' situation as it is depicted by the evangelists. As a series of spiritual reflections, it is meant to lead readers closer to the risen Christ, not to the historical figure of Jesus.

Third, consider how Guardini's personality may have affected a text's outlook and tone. Guardini was a highly sensitive and intuitive individual. As such, he was attuned to an organization's inadequacies as well as to its merits. Thus, *The Church and the Catholic* illumines ways in which the church nurtures our individual and communal lives, and it also speaks of the church as a flawed institution, indeed, as "Christ's cross." As already mentioned, Guardini struggled throughout his life with depression; he wrote *Schwermut* (Depression) as a personal testimony on how to live with despondency and possibly even to make it a source of creativity. Guardini's sadness comes through his writings. His despondency during his last years influences the tone of *The Church of the Lord.*

Fourth, locate the text in its original setting in German history and in church history. During the Weimar Republic, seeking to offset what he perceived to be an ethos of individualism, he emphasized the social character of human life in *The Church and the Catholic.* During the Third Reich, alarmed by the Nazi state's disregard for human rights, he focused in *The Person and the World* on the sacredness of the individual person. Or, to take another example, the interpretation of the Bible in *The Lord* is problematic because Guardini wrote this book before the Catholic Church allowed its scholars to use historical-critical methods of biblical interpretation. In *The Lord,* Guardini used John's Gospel as the lens through which he interprets the Gospels of Matthew, Mark, and Luke. Instead, he should have read each Gospel as a coherent literary and theological whole in itself.

Fifth, see each text in relation to Guardini's entire literary corpus. Readers who limit themselves to Guardini's address of 1964 at Mainz on the liturgical renewal and to *The Church of the Lord* may wrongly conclude that Guardini opposed the Second Vatican Council. Beginning with *The Spirit of the Liturgy* in 1918, he diligently worked for the liturgical renewal eventually embraced by Vatican II.

Sixth and finally, appreciate how Guardini's writings reflect the intellectual and spiritual orientation of St. Augustine. Texts in the Augustinian heritage — for example, Blaise Pascal's *Pensées* — envision the heights to which God calls human beings, while they also illumine the human failure to attain those heights. When presented with a half-full glass of water, Augustinians notice the size of the glass and how much water is missing; they neglect to note how much water is already in the glass. In *The Lord,* Guardini reiterates that God calls men and women to share in Christ's life, and he illumines the ambiguities of the human heart. But he is silent about human accomplishments over the centuries.

The writings of Romano Guardini attest in various ways and in varying degrees to God's grandeur and to humanity's potential greatness. Like diamonds in the light, these books and essays radiate the divine and human realities with which we live. In fact, they have so many facets that they invite numerous interpretations. In his eulogy for Guardini in 1968, Karl Rahner said that Guardini's writings "were meant to serve only the eternal in man, his original and authentic relationship to God, as it is lived and not merely talked about. All this in countless pages telling of man and thus seeking to tell of God who is the true mystery of man." From another perspective, however, the primary contribution of Guardini's work was Christological, as was pointed out by Cardinal Joseph Ratzinger in 1996: "As we are taught by Guardini, the essence of Christianity is not an idea, not a system of thought, not a plan of action. The essence of Christianity is a Person: Jesus Christ himself. That which is essential is the One who is essential. To become truly real means to come to know Jesus Christ and to learn from him what it means to be human." Complementing each other, these statements by Rahner and Ratzinger attest to the richness of Guardini's thought. All commentators agree that Guardini time and again shed new light on the drama in which God's heart draws to itself our hearts, which remain restless until they rest in God.*

*I am grateful to Sue Rozeboom for her critical reading of earlier versions of this introduction and the five chapters of this book.

Selected Literature in English on Romano Guardini

Farrugia, Mario. "Guardini, Romano (1885–1968)." In *Dictionary of Fundamental Theology,* ed. René Latourelle and Rino Fisichella, 403–6. New York: Crossroad, 1994.

Hellwig, Monika. "A Catholic Scholar's Journey through the Twentieth Century." In *Faith and the Intellectual Life,* ed. James L. Heft, 71–85. Notre Dame, Ind.: University of Notre Dame Press, 1996.

Hill, Roland. "Spiritual Liberator," *The Catholic World Report* 1 (June 1992): 52–55.

Krieg, Robert A. *Catholic Theologians in Nazi Germany,* 107–30. New York: Continuum, 2004.

———. *Romano Guardini: A Precursor of Vatican II.* Notre Dame, Ind.: University of Notre Dame Press, 1997.

———, ed. *Romano Guardini: Proclaiming the Sacred in a Modern World.* Chicago: Liturgy Training Publications, 1995.

———. "Romano Guardini's Theology of the Human Person," *Theological Studies* 59 (1998): 457–74.

Kuehn, Heinz R. *The Essential Guardini: An Anthology of the Writings of Romano Guardini.* Chicago: Liturgy Training Publications, 1997.

Kuehn, Regina. "Romano Guardini: Teacher of Teachers." In *How Firm a Foundation: Leaders of the Liturgical Movement,* ed. Robert Tuzik, 36–49. Chicago: Liturgy Training Publications, 1990.

Misner, Paul. "Guardini, Romano." In *New Catholic Encyclopedia,* 2nd ed., vol. 6, 550. Washington, D.C.: Catholic University of America, 2003.

Rahner, Karl. "Romano Guardini's Successor." In *I Remember,* 73–75. Trans. Harvey D. Egan, New York: Crossroad, 1985.

———. "Thinker and Christian: Obituary of Romano Guardini" (1968). *Opportunities for Faith,* 127–31. Trans. Edward Quinn. New York: Seabury Press, 1974.

Ratzinger, Joseph Cardinal. "Guardini on Christ in Our Century." Trans. John M. Haas. *Crisis* 14 (June 1996): 14–15.

Chapter 1

Living in Relationship with God

O God, you are my God, I seek you,
my soul thirsts for you.
—Psalm 63:1

When children are learning to walk, they resist their parents' efforts to help them. They push adults away as they crawl, run, and climb stairs. This drive for independence stays with us, and makes us reluctant to get close to other people and even to God. According to Romano Guardini, we desire intimacy with God, but we hold back from God because we wrongly fear that closeness to God will stifle our freedom. We must experience a paradox: trust in God does not keep us infantile but enables us to mature and simultaneously to remain faithful to God and others. The first step to freedom is to surrender to "the higher power."

As Guardini describes in his memoirs, he struggled for many years to come to a true sense of himself and his calling. Drawing on this painful journey, he reflected throughout his life on the complexities of being human. In particular, he considered how every man or woman can move to self-acceptance, to becoming an "I" in relation to God and to other men and women. Near the end of his life, Guardini considered how God offers each of us wisdom, "the gift of being able to distinguish between what is worthwhile and what is valueless."

GOD'S WORD TO EACH OF US (1964)

Last night — it was well toward morning when dreams often come — a dream came to me. I do not recall any longer what occurred in it, but something was said either to me or by me; I do not remember which. It was said that when a human being is born, he or she receives a word from God. What is said is important. It is not only an inspiration, but a word. This word is uttered in the infant's very being; it is a guide for everything that will happen in one's life. This word is both a strength and a liability. A mandate and a promise. A guard and a challenge. Everything that then occurs in the person's life is somehow related to the realization of this word. A human life is an elucidation and a fulfillment of the divine word which influences all aspects of this life. This word is spoken to each human being. It understands each of us, and comes into harmony with us. This word is perhaps the basis on which God will eventually judge each human being. —BML, 20

FINDING ONE'S CENTER (1945)

If young people were to read my memoirs, they would surely be amazed that someone could be as unclear about himself as I had been. The primary cause for this confusion lay above all in me, in the complexity of my personal being which only slowly found its center point.

What brought about my own religious life was also what put great pressure on my religious life until my university years.

I was always anxious and very scrupulous. For a young person, this condition is more difficult than an easygoing sense of life. An easygoing sense of life is at least a life, while the self-preoccupation of the anxious conscience is destructive. Help for this condition can properly come only from an older person who sees the anxiety. As a youth, however, I did not meet such a person. Added to this condition for me was the tendency toward depression which later became acute. Nevertheless, this tendency was also a source of creativity for me.

My scrupulosity and tendency toward depression could have led even in my early years to an intense inner life, full of strong experiences. But this did not happen. When I look back on my life, I am not able to see the entire time up until my university years. Nothing comes to me from my early childhood memories — memories which usually make the beginning of an autobiography worthwhile. I do not want to suggest that those years were empty. What unfolded later in my life must have had its roots in my early years. But everything from my childhood lies as though under water. I have never had the sense of a happy childhood nor the desire to return to my childhood. I would not like to return to my childhood. I wish to add, however, that my parents truly loved us, and we them. We four brothers were closely united despite all conflicts, tensions, and difficulties, and it has remained that way even to this day.

When I finally arrived in Freiburg in 1906, I experienced an indescribable despondency. The prospect of becoming a priest threw me into a dark depression. I no longer understood myself. Today I know that what expressed itself in this despondency was the resistance of an entirely unlived out nature to the necessary deprivations of the priesthood. Also, since birth, I have borne the inheritance of the depression that my mother experienced. Such an inheritance is not in itself bad; it is the ballast that gives a ship its ability to travel the deep seas. I do not believe that there is creativity and a deep relationship to life without having a disposition toward depression. A person cannot eliminate it, but must include it in his or her life. As part of this, one must accept it in an innermost way from God, and must try to transform it into a good for other people.

I did not have this insight into depression when I went to Freiburg. After I arrived there, the flood waters of depression climbed so high in me that I thought I was sinking, and I considered putting an end to my life. I found peace in a few specific places; this sounds pathetic, but it is true. In Freiburg's cathedral, the Münster, the altar for the reservation of the Blessed Sacrament stood to the right of the main altar. When I knelt on the steps of this side altar, the despondency lessened — only to return soon afterward. How long the depression continued I no longer know. In my memory it seems endless. It was in fact not more than a couple of weeks. But it is not only the external duration which makes time seem long.

One day I was going to St. Odilien Church, where a natural spring of water bubbles up, which is a pleasure to watch. On the return way, on the beautiful street that passes the Carthusian house, I prayed the rosary. The sadness lessened, and I became peaceful. It was my first real encounter with this prayer, which I later prayed so frequently. Since that moment I have never doubted my call to the priesthood. The dark flow of depression has always continued in my life, and more than once it has climbed very high. It was clear to me, however, that I was being called to the priesthood, and I have kept this conviction into the present.

I must say more about Wilhelm Koch, who was one of our professors of theology in Tübingen. Above all, I must recall that Koch was the person who freed me from the demands of scrupulosity. As I said earlier, scrupulosity had afflicted me since my childhood; during my first semester in Tübingen, it became unbearable. I attribute this senseless self-preoccupation in good part to the fact that my nerves were so sensitive and have never entirely healed. Scrupulosity is connected, too, to my tendency toward depression, and it can to a certain extent have a positive effect because it makes one serious. But it can also destroy judgment and energy, to say nothing of the danger of inner panic that can drive anxious persons in the wrong direction so that they throw aside all moral and religious restraints.

In any event, Koch had the custom of hearing the confessions of a few students. Some of us — Karl Neundörfer, Josef Weiger, and I — asked him for this favor, and he agreed. He heard someone's confession in the following manner. At the agreed upon time, the confessee arrived at Koch's room, and walked back and forth with him in the room. This allowed the penitent to tell all that he had on his heart — whether about studies or practical matters, religious questions or moral issues — and to say what he thought about these things. Then Koch put on his stole, asked the penitent to give a summary of all that was discussed, and then gave the absolution. In this way, I experienced what a wonderful source of life the sacrament of reconciliation can be when it is performed properly. I learned to stand at a distance from my anxieties, to distinguish unimportant concerns from important ones, and to see the appropriate tasks of my personal and religious formation.

Since Koch was a good person, he offered us some advice that we followed. At that time, we had no knowledge of human sexuality, and he saw how this ignorance burdened us. So he sent each of us to a professor of psychiatry, who was empathetic to us and recommended a good book about sexual matters. This endeavor was a bit risky since Professor G. was not a Christian. The book was entitled *Die sexuelle Frage* (The sexual Question), by Forel. It treated sexual matters with a matter-of-factness and detail that served us well. We read the book aloud together and found that the whole subject became demystified.

These steps to inner freedom had the net effect of turning the semester into a good experience. I cannot say that my anxiety totally disappeared. Since it is really part of my very makeup, it always runs as a possibility beneath the surface of my life. I have attained, however, a critical distance from it and now am able to distinguish among its demands and assess each of them.

In the course of my last year at the University of Bonn, I was invited to accept a faculty position at Bonn in practical theology and liturgical studies. I had the intuition, however, that I should not deviate from my inner sense of direction, and therefore that I should not take this position. As I mention this, I would like to say that, since the awakening of my spiritual life, I had come to trust my inner orientation, and I have made my life's various decisions concerning professional, spiritual, and personal matters on the basis of this inner sense of direction.

—BML, 57, 61, 76–77, 81–82, 35

At the age of thirty-eight, Romano Guardini as a professor at the University of Berlin and as a chaplain to Quickborn developed key elements of his Christian humanism in his lectures and sermons. He gave much attention to the challenge of personal development.

BECOMING A PERSON (1925)

A human person is not solely an individual entity, not solely a private reality. Along with having autonomy, each human being exists in relation to other people. For the Christian, the social aspect of human life springs from the fact that the true or proper "person," God — of whom a human being is an image — is both individual and social. God has revealed to us that his personal being exists in a communal reality. The first divine person is the one who is "Father," hence, one within a community. The second divine person is "Son." The third divine person is "Spirit," who is community-affirming love. The communal reality of God is not secondary to the individuality of each divine person, rather the autonomy of each divine person is grounded in the unchangeable uniqueness of each person within God's communal being. The divine community is constituted by these unchangeable persons. We can understand God's personal reality only by starting with our experience as human persons. However, in the order of being, the divine persons are the primary reality, and human persons are reflections of the divine being. Thus for Christians, God's self-revelation is the religious basis for insights into the personal existence of every human being. —LLB, 152

BEING IN THE WORLD (1928)

"The world" consists not of things in themselves alone, but of that which comes about as we encounter these things. When we see things and experience them, when we approach things and come in contact with them, we become involved with them, dwell and live with them. What comes about then is the authentic world. The world is not only outside of us and also not only within us; it is that reality which is interiorly unfolding outside of us and which is also reaching out from within us. It is this world that God intends since God creates both things and human beings.

There are not "things" and "human beings" in general. There is this particular cypress tree that has grown up here—at this spot on the slope where the breeze strikes it every evening. And there is this specific human being, me, who walks near the cypress. There is also my life as it has unfolded until now and as it includes what I have inherited and somehow carry in me. I now walk along the slope. I see the cypress, and an encounter occurs between the cypress and me. If I approach the cypress appropriately, who knows how the cypress may respond? Is it only "make believe" when in folk tales a tree sees people and speaks to them? In any case, the "world" comes about, at this moment, in the encounter between the cypress and me. When human beings truly encounter things, the world emerges as God intends it. This world is always new. —TAO, 18–19

During the Third Reich (1933–45), as Hitler was depriving Germans of their civil rights and human dignity, Guardini highlighted the sacred character of every human being.

OBSERVATIONS ABOUT HUMAN LIFE (1937)

We cannot bring forth justice if we want justice alone. We can be just only when we act from a point which lies beyond justice. We cannot oppose injustice when we seek to preserve only the norm of justice. We must act out of the power of love, which lacks nothing and is gracious and creative. Then true justice becomes possible. —HE, pt. 2, ch. 1, p. 92

Satan is neither an abstract principle nor a primal force, but a fallen creature, estranged because of rebellion. Satan seeks to establish a desperate kingdom of appearances and disorder. Satan has power only because we have sinned, and he is a power against the human heart which exists in truth and humility. . . . Jesus exists in a struggle against Satan and aims at entering into our souls, ensnared by Satan, in order to enlighten our consciences, to awaken our hearts, and to release our good energies. —HE, pt. 2, ch. 7, pp. 130–31

Between God and us stands a wall: sin. As the Holy One, God is angry at us and rejects us. Yet the Holy Spirit takes down this wall. The Holy Spirit arises out of God's heart. To be more accurate, the Holy Spirit is God's heart, God's eternal inner life. The Holy Spirit brings God's divine life to us and restores us to what we were in the beginning. There comes about in us not a mixture of sin and holiness but a new existence in an unspeakable inner life. We who are creatures share a community of life, a community of heart with God. We know that this new existence has taken place not because we have reasoned to it but because we believe in God's word.

—HE, pt. 2, ch. 12, p. 169

Justice is good; it is the basis of human existence. There is however something beyond justice: the free opening of one's heart to kindness. Justice is clear; but when it goes a step further it becomes cold. But kindness — genuine, heartfelt kindness, arising from one's character — warms and frees. Justice orders things, but kindness brings them forth. Justice does what suffices, what is. By contrast, kindness creates something new. In justice the human spirit attains the satisfaction of good order. But out of kindness springs the joy of a creative life.

—HE, pt. 4, ch. 7, p. 310

THE INVIOLABLE SELF (1939)

Personal existence means that I can ultimately be possessed by no one else because I belong to myself. I could have lived in an age when slavery was permitted so that someone could buy other human beings and have control over them. An owner exercised power, however, not over these slaves as persons but over some of their physical and psychological elements. Moreover, the owner did so falsely, regarding the slaves as animals.

A proprietary relationship does not extend to the reality of personal existence.... To be a person means that I can be used by no one; I am an end in myself. I may work at a job in which the managers treat me solely as a functionary in a machine. If so, then it is only my performance or output which they make use of; they do not make use of me as a person.

The personal existence of a man or woman is threatened when the individual is loosened from those realities and norms that safeguard personal existence; among these are justice and love. Human beings deteriorate as persons when they relinquish justice. This personal erosion takes place not only when people act unjustly, but also when they do not pursue justice. The pursuit of justice entails both the acknowledgment that something or someone is its own reality and also the readiness to protect the rights of this reality and the relationships appropriate to it.

—WU, ch. 1, sec. 4, pp. 93–94, 97

As West Germany became a vibrant democracy, Guardini elucidated the link between personal development and belief in God.

THE RELATIONAL SELF (1952)

The likeness of human beings to God penetrates all aspects of human life. The truth and mystery of this assertion is evident in the fundamental ways in which men and women exist, and in a basic understanding of human life.

At the beginning of his *Confessions,* St. Augustine gives a permanently valid expression of this human reality when he writes, "You have made us for yourself, O God." This statement is meant not to be primarily enthusiastic or inspirational but to be descriptive. God has created human beings in a personal relationship with God, and without this relationship we can neither exist nor make sense of our lives. We do not truly understand human life if we think that men and women can live as self-enclosed individuals. On the contrary, a human being exists through a primary relationship — a relationship from God and to God. This relationship with God is not secondary to someone's life as though the individual could exist apart from it. In fact, every human being lives in relationship with God.

Men and women can relate to other human beings in various types of relationships: colleagues, friends, and assistants. Human beings mature in these relationships, but they do not primarily depend on them. Someone remains a human being even without knowledge of this or that other person, or without helping a specific individual. A person's relationship with God is of a different sort. A bridge is the arch which a builder constructs from one bank of a river to the other bank. It cannot be said that this structure is a bridge if it does not reach from one side of the river to the other. Something similar must be said in any discussion about human existence and God. A human being exists only in relationship with God. The movement "from God" and "to God" occurs in every human life.

This reality becomes clearer when we focus on that which differentiates human beings from all other earthly creatures, namely, personal existence. That someone is a person means that he or she exists in a unique way. Someone may act on his or her own initiative and may have self-control. If asked, "Who has done this or that?," the person can answer, "I have," thereby accepting responsibility for this action. God has created each human being in this way. However, God has created human beings not only so that they exist in themselves but also so that something more can come about. God has made human beings to be God's "other," God's "you." Further, God has determined that God should be the "other," the proper "you," of human beings. The human essence is anchored in this "I-you" or "I-Thou" relationship with God. It is only because God has created men and women to live in this relationship of I-you with God that they can enter into personal relationships with one another. That one human being can say to another, "I am aware of you,... I respect you," is possible only because God has granted to each of us the ability to say to God, the Lord, "You are my creator,... I pray to you." —MEN, 48–50

SELF-ACCEPTANCE (1953)

Self-acceptance is an act of asceticism. I must renounce my wish to be other than I am, to be someone other than who I am. The persistence of the human desire to be something other than oneself is clear in the ancient myths and fairy tales, which are found among all peoples, that recount how a man or woman is changed into something else—into a star in the heavens, an animal, a monster, or a stone....

At the heart of everything human is the act in which I accept myself. I must agree to be who I am. Agree to have the qualities that I in fact have. Agree to exist within the limits that were given to me.

I cannot explain how I am as I am. I cannot understand why I must be so. I cannot make sense of my life according to laws of nature or history, for my personal existence is not a necessity but a fact. It is simply the most decisive fact for me. It is how it is, and cannot be otherwise. It is, though it also could not be. Nevertheless, who I am defines my whole existence.

All of this means that I cannot explain my identity, nor can I somehow prove myself. Rather I must accept myself. And the clarity and courage for this self-acceptance shapes all that exists in my life.

I cannot fulfill this challenge to be myself solely through my own efforts alone. I can accept myself only in relation to something or someone higher — and with this recognition we are in the realm of faith. Faith means here that I understand my finitude in relation to the highest reality, in relation to God's will.

God is a reality and a necessity. God is meaningfully grounded in God's very self and needs no explanation. The explanation of God is God alone. God is so because God is so. And God exists because God is God. God is the absolute self-comprehending One. We must accept that the "self," whose understanding is spoken of here, is God's.

This God is the Lord, and God is the Lord because of the divine essence. This means not only that God is the Lord of creation, but also and primarily that God is the Lord in God's very self. God abides in divine sovereignty. This mystery is conveyed in the name which God communicated to us. At the start of salvation history there is the vision on Mount Horeb. "But Moses said to God, 'If I come to the Israelites and say to them, "The God of your ancestors has sent me to you," and they ask me, "What is his name?" What shall I say to them?' God said to Moses, 'I am who I am.' He said further, 'Thus you shall say to the Israelites, "I am has sent me to you"' " (Exod. 3:13–14). What is the meaning of the name that God has told us? It means: I am the One who exists in reality and power, and I am now acting.... This name also means: I accept no name from the world but receive my name from myself alone.... Further, in its deepest sense this name expresses God's message: My name is the manner in which I am I myself. I alone exist in this way, simultaneously in pure necessity and complete freedom.

This God is the One who created me. We remain in this awareness: God is the One who has given me to myself. With this recognition, my questioning comes to an end. It is in relation to this acknowledgment that one might ask, why has God given me to myself, as this individual, here and now? But this question makes no sense; it shows I have not truly recognized who and what God is. I could answer, God has created me because it is correct in the whole of the world, or because I should do this or that, or because it was meaningful to create me. But this answer says not more, but less, than simply to say, God made me because God wanted to create me.

A highly respected account of how a human being comes to personal existence is Dantes's *Divine Comedy.* This great work tells of the journey from earth through hell and all its depths, through the place of purification with all of its stages, through the spheres of heaven into the ecstasy of God. At the conclusion, one reads how the mystery of Christ is revealed to the traveler; it is through Jesus Christ that our humanity is assumed into the existence of the Son of God. In the presence of Christ, the traveler apprehends what is situated not only beyond everything earthly but also beyond himself. He now knows who Christ is and also who he himself, Dante, is. He also knows now all that God intends for him.

The reality of our relationship with God is profound, even when I understand it properly.

Who I am I can grasp only in relation to what is beyond me. No; it is better to say that I can understand myself only in relation to the One who has given me me. I cannot understand myself only in relation to myself. Questions about human life which use the word "why" and the word "I" cannot be answered by an individual alone. These questions include: Why am I as I am? Why can I have only what I have? Why do I exist? These questions can be answered only in relation to God.

—AS, 17, 18, 20–22, 30–31

CREATED IN GOD'S IMAGE (1963)

Human beings exist in the image of God. But how do they resemble God? According to the Bible, God governs creation on his own authority, and God has simultaneously willed that human beings should also govern it. It is important to understand the meaning of this "also." God governs by his very nature because God is God. Human beings govern, however, by grace because God gives them the ability to do so. Insofar as human beings govern the world according to God's will, they direct the world to obey God as well. By understanding, judging, acting, and forming, men and women fashion creation into God's kingdom. Insofar as human beings exist in the service of the highest Lord, the world becomes the kingdom of God. This then is how men and women should exist in the image of God.

If human beings had remained obedient to God, they would have become increasingly similar to God. They would have shaped the world more and more perfectly and offered it back to God in increasingly purer love. But they rebelled against God. They tried to govern the world by their own powers and to make it for themselves. As a result, they became enslaved to the world. They betrayed the true Lord and regarded the world as their god. Thus they generated the gods, the concentrations of the power which gained control over human beings after they abandoned God. Human beings, who should exist in the image of God, have become similar to gods. What this means is evident when one looks not only at the gods like Apollo and Athena but also at the dark, terrifying, and horrible figures whom human beings have regarded as gods. When we take note of these gods, we become disillusioned enough to see the empty coldness, the anonymous "it," of even the most attractive Olympian figures.

This is a truth that we must take very seriously. What we are is ultimately defined not by us but by the God or the gods in whom we believe. Rationalists insist that we make our gods according to our own character, disposition, and needs. To an extent, this is true. But it is more the case that we become similar to what we believe in. When we believe in nothing, then we find that we have no identity, that we have nothing at the core of our being.

When I am conscious, for example, of how God has created me by his call to me so that I experience myself as an individual who is called by God, when I see the different situations of my life as modes which express God's call to me and see my responses to these situations as my answers to this divine call, then I find that my personal identity becomes stronger, more confident, and freer. In this process, I discover myself richer and more connected to what's eternal.

By contrast, when I think of God as pantheism does, that is, as the universal spirit, or as the primal mystery, or as the essence of the world, then I become not a clear and responsible self or "you," but only a vague, indefinite being. Indeed, this indefiniteness penetrates my innermost being and deprives me of the ability to say yes or no to the decisive questions of human existence. . . .

The most basic decision of our lives consists in acknowledging who God is in relation to the gods and godlessness of politics and culture and poetry and other things. Only because God has defined human beings in their very essence are we what we are. Only by receiving ourselves from God do we remain sure of ourselves. Only because we are addressed by God can each of us really say "I." For the whole existence of each of us is nothing other than our answer to God's creative call: "You, exist!"

What then is wisdom? It concerns how life can attain its proper meaning, how it can participate in that which endures. Wisdom ensures that at the end of life we do not stand with empty hands. It relies on the gift of being able to distinguish between what is worthwhile and what is valueless, between what lasts forever and what passes away, what is genuine and what is phoney. According to Psalm 90, the distinction which is the basis of all other distinctions is this: God alone is God, eternally existing, holy and living, and human beings are only human, created and passing. Yet human beings are capable of acknowledging the truth and experiencing what has true value. They are obligated to pursue the good and to be responsible to God for how they use their lives....

When we ask, "What should I do? Wisdom, advise me!" Wisdom answers: "You must learn to distinguish. You must bring into your life that which God values — not that which is seemingly impressive or exciting, but that which is authentic."

And what is authentic? Wisdom answers: "The good!" When I have fulfilled an obligation, although is was unpleasant for me, the situation changes, the issue no longer exists, but something remains: the good that was done. This good is what God values.

Or when I act with love toward someone whom I do not like, seeking to understand and to help the person, I fulfill a divine commandment and something comes about which lasts. Surrounding this act are many things that fall away: the encounter itself is over, the stimulus ceases, the individuals involved — both the other person and I — will eventually die. But at this moment I conveyed love, and this love is what remains since this is what God values.

Or I may have a friend who, like every human being, possesses good personal traits and also unattractive ones. Much about the person brings me delight, but some things turn me off. It is easy to say to myself, I will accept my friend's delightful qualities but not the unattractive ones. However, wisdom says: "You cannot do that! You cannot be selective about a person's traits for all of them belong to this individual. Your friend's best qualities are connected with his or her deepest weaknesses. If you do not accept everything, then you lose this person." Acceptance of another person requires patience. God values patience. God is patient with me and with every person. You too must be so, and permanence will come to your friendship. You may seek to influence your friend, trying to encourage some qualities and to lessen others. But first you must say yes to the whole person.

That which is most beautiful in the world is brought about when one person loves another. I do not mean passion, although this has its good aspects. Rather, I mean the wonderful phenomenon in which one human being, who by nature is self-oriented, opens to another person, and welcomes the beloved into his or her heart. When we love in this way, we make the beloved as important to us as we are to ourselves, and perhaps even more important. As a result, the one person feels secure in the other.

Wisdom says, however, that it is foolish to try to force one person to respond to another's love. It is foolish to demand that this love should exist. To insist that this love should last forever. To get demanding when the other withdraws. To want to somehow buy love with special deeds and favors.... All of these efforts would be foolish because love can exist only in freedom. It must be a gift and must always be given anew. If love has been given over ten long years, it does not mean that it will necessarily be given during an eleventh year. To be sure, love has the desire to persist because it possesses an eternal character. But love unfolds not out of necessity but always anew out of freedom. For this reason, love dies when it is not honored with freedom; it dies when one person senses that the other person is taking the love for granted and is no longer working at loving well. While one person cannot compel another to reciprocate in love, a person can nourish love and nurture it with attentiveness and courtesy. Then love can flourish. When someone understands all of this, the person has attained wisdom.

—WP, ch. 3, pp. 146–49; ch. 12, pp. 239, 240–42

During his last years, Guardini wrote a manuscript on Christian discipleship; this book was published after his death.

IN DIALOGUE WITH GOD (1976)

The creative act, which revelation presents to us as the basis for being a person and for existing as a specific person in the nonpersonal world, presupposes an I-you dialogue between a human being and God — a dialogue that God initiates. The book of Genesis speaks in images. It is not a scientific presentation but a proclamation springing from the Holy Spirit. When we correctly understand the verses that speak of the creation of the world (Gen. 1–2), we see how the creation of nonpersonal things — earth, sea, light, plants, and animals — utilizes the image of crafted realities. God "made" these things, in that God ordered that they should exist. Even in the creation of human beings such an image appears: God forms the human body out of the earth as a potter forms vessels on a wheel. What makes a man or woman a human being—namely, the life of the soul, the interiority of the spirit, the freedom of the person—comes about however through God's breath and through God's speaking the name, "Adam," which may mean "human being out of the earth." Here God's creative act itself takes on a personal character so that we may say that a divine call creates the personal existence of every human being. God calls: "You"; each of us responds by becoming an authentic human person. The personal existence of every human being is in its deepest sense one's answer to God's call, "You."

When Genesis says further that human beings exist in the "image" of God (Gen. 1:26–27), it is assumed that this similarity is a man or woman's personal existence. The fact is that each human being not only answers God's call, but is the answer itself to this call. A human being exists only in the I-you relation with God. It is the ontological order in which someone lives. In light of this reality, we become aware of the absurdity of the assertion that God does not exist. —EC, 475–76

A PRAYER ON OUR RELATIONSHIP WITH GOD (1948)

O God, you have created us and wonderfully established our being. You have desired that we should live according to the principles of your wisdom, so that our energies unfold in ever new encounters with these principles and become empowered for their proper freedom. Our interactions with the things of this world should prepare us for our encounter with you. You are the only One. For each of us, you are the ultimate "you," the only One who truly fulfills us. We are orientated to you, and only in you will our true essence come to fulfillment as you have desired it.

You are the truth that gives validity to every finite truth. You are the holiness that makes every good thing sacred. You are the heart for which we long. "You have created us for you, and our heart is restless until it rests in you."

My value is anchored in the respect that you, O God, have for me. My honor is based on your honor. If I were to leave you, I would be like one of those people of whom the apostle says: "For if any are hearers of the Word and not doers, they are like those who look at themselves in a mirror; for they look at themselves and, on going away, immediately forget what they were like" (James 1:23). You are the sacred mirror in which I alone am certain of my eternal countenance and aware of my obligations. If I were to depart from you, I would be separated from myself. Moreover, if I were to depart from you, this world's powers, which are meant to serve me, would become masters over me.

Embrace me in a sacred intimacy with you. Make my heart incorruptible so that it can perceive what leads away from you. Just as emergency medical teams immediately awaken when life is endangered, so strengthen my innermost self to go immediately against everything that would separate me from you. Amen. —TG, ch. 7, pp. 18–19

Chapter 2

The Living God

For you, O Lord, are the most high over all the earth;
you are exalted far above all gods. —Psalm 96:4

The question is not: Does God exist? It is instead: Which God or gods do I worship? To varying degrees, we adore idols, specifically, an addiction, an unhealthy need for someone, fear of an authority figure, an anxiety about money, a drive to manipulate others. In the course of our days — if all goes well — we gradually set aside our false gods and trust more and more in the God of Jesus Christ. Romano Guardini tried to show the paradox that the true God embraces us and simultaneously sets us free to become the "other" whom God intends.

In Guardini's judgment, there is no standard way to God. As a youth, Guardini himself was guided by his mother and a childless married couple who took an interest in him. As he searched for God, he learned the importance of following one's conscience and also experienced both God's closeness and absence. He observed, too, that believers who set out to defend "orthodoxy" frequently in fact misunderstand and misrepresent the truths contained in the church's teachings. During his last years, Guardini reflected on God's incomprehensibility and the reality of evil.

A JOURNEY TOWARD GOD (1945)

When it came to religious belief, my parents were faithful Catholics. My father held a mildly skeptical outlook on religion, which is very common among Italian men. While he went to church every Sunday, he never spoke about religious matters. My mother was pious in a very interior and ascetical manner. I remember how on weekday mornings she would come to our bed — after she had been to Mass and received communion, which was seldom received in those days — and kiss my brothers and me. I found her action to be mysterious and sacred. We took for granted our religious practices of morning and evening prayers, attendance at church on Sundays, and the like. We spoke about religious matters only when there was a specific reason for doing so.

My teacher of religion in high school was talented; he held a doctorate in theology. But he was absolutely unintelligible when he tried to teach. I learned nothing from him, and still less did he awaken in me a genuine interest in religious matters.

Especially important for me was my relationship with two people whom I met shortly before I graduated from high school. They were Wilhelm Schleussner, teacher of German and history at Mainz's technical high school, and his wife, Josephine. They were childless, and they welcomed many people into their lives. Through a school friend, I was introduced to them and began to visit them, at first only from time to time, but eventually very frequently. I visited them so often that I now wonder how both of them, who had their own work to do, could have given me so much of their time. Herr Schleussner was a convert and had intense religious interests. Above all, he knew the German mystics and eventually, using the pseudonym Brother Bardo, edited the book *Deutsche Gebete* (German Prayers), published by Matthias Grünewald.

Frau Schleussner was even more significant for me than he was. From her parents, she had acquired a fine education, understood Latin, and had learned Spanish so that she could read in the original the writings of St. Teresa of Avila, whom she loved. She shared her spiritual life with her husband and helped him with his writing. At the same time, motivated by a concern for others and self-renunciation, she did wonderful work through Mainz's Catholic service organization. This involvement showed that she did not belong to high society. She was full of love and life, and I enjoyed being with her. I experienced with Frau Schleussner the respect which a young person can have for a much older, spiritually profound, and humanly very fine woman. To this relationship was added what I did not know at the beginning: not only did she lead an intense religious life, but she also had religious experiences. In her presence, I felt something unusual in the sense of a goodness and interior life which never entangled or overwhelmed someone but was always helpful to others. I discussed my religious issues with Herr and Frau Schleussner and became conscious of the fact that I wanted to speak chiefly with Frau Schleussner. Hence it was wonderful when I could meet only with her and tell her what I had on my heart. —BML, 60, 67–68

In his teaching and pastoral ministry, Guardini discussed the mystery of God and simultaneously shed light on the ways in which people experience God in the contemporary world.

GOD AND CONSCIENCE (1928)

Conscience is first of all that sense on the basis of which I respond to what is good and know for myself what the good is. Conscience is absolutely significant. What is ultimate in my life exists in union with my conscience. Conscience should be acted on. In this action what is ultimate is affirmed.

Conscience is also the sense by which I apprehend a situation's meaning and what is good in this situation. It is that by which I choose what is good here and now. The act of conscience is therefore that act in which I look deeply into a specific situation and understand what is right and good in this situation.

Conscience is therefore also that point at which the eternal enters into time. It is the birthplace of history. History — which is entirely different from a natural process — is enkindled in conscience. History means that the eternal occurs in time through the free acts of men and women.

Conscience is our sense of the good, and it is also our orientation toward God. As we are attentive to our sense of what we should do — to our awareness, our decisions, and our conscience — we reach religious ground. Conscience in its depths involves a person's "soul," one's "inner voice." Conscience at its highest moment engages the Holy Spirit. In all of its facets, conscience concerns religious, spiritual reality. Hence, conscience is our orientation toward God — toward the living God who remains near to us and sets challenges before us.

God embraces us, surrounds us, enters into us. God abides at the innermost point of our existence. There where our very being borders on the edge of nothingness, God holds us in his hands. There God speaks to us. Not as a general power, not as a mere law. Not as an "it," but as an "I," to whom each of us relates as a "you." This God is the creator and the Lord of all. . . .

God speaks to us both from within ourselves through the voice of our conscience and also from outside ourselves in the seeming coincidence of people and events. The divine word from within us clarifies the divine word from outside us, and vice versa. A person's ethical life arises out of the continually new challenges coming from the interplay of the inner word and the outer word. In relation to this interaction, it is important to reflect on Christ's words: "Do not worry about tomorrow; tomorrow will take care of itself. Sufficient for a day is its own evil" (Matt. 6:34). And further, "Give us this day our daily bread" (Matt. 5:11). The interplay of the word within us and the word outside us simultaneously engages the deepest elements of our human existence and the riches of divine revelation.

We must purify our inner lives. We must become attentive and ready. We must fulfill our obligations, interact with the situations in which we find ourselves, and satisfy their demands to the best of our ability. We must open ourselves to our experiences and live our lives in response to the events that come to us; we must not turn aside. Conscience assures us that the resolution of a situation will come about as we make our way through it. We must undertake delightful tasks and difficult ones, even those that are very difficult. In short, we must enter into life as it comes to us from God. We must allow ourselves to learn from life — from our lives! Stretching us, reprimanding us, enabling us to see.

We must continually pray for clarity of conscience. In this regard, Cardinal John Henry Newman has written this prayer:

> I need you, God. You teach me, day after day, after each day's challenges and needs. Give me, O Lord, the clarity of conscience that senses your inspiration, and strengthen me to heed it. My ears are deaf; I cannot hear your voice. My eyes are cloudy; I cannot see your signs. You alone can open my hearing and clear my sight; you alone can purify

and renew my heart. Teach me to sit at your feet and to listen to your word. Amen.

—RM, 53–54, 69, 72–74, 90–91

As Germans struggled to survive during the twelve years of Nazi terror and the aftermath of the war, Guardini called attention to God's activity in human life, a divine presence that at times can feel like an absence.

GOD'S ACTIVITY IN OUR LIVES (1933)

God exists in movement. God lives, and God's living is love. I begin to understand God's love when I see it directed not to the world in general but to me. God is acting in love toward me. When Holy Scripture says, "Come, Lord," it is referring not to an image or idea of God but to the living God. This thought should not confuse us: God is present everywhere. Surely God is everywhere; everything exists through God, and God sustains everything. Nevertheless, God comes to each of us. God always comes to us. God is the One coming to us — coming to human beings, and through human beings coming to the world which God will eventually raise into eternal newness.

Christian existence is authentic human existence. The Christian is the kind of person whom God intends. There is no "merely natural" human being. Each human being whom God has in mind comes to full existence when this man or this woman, who has been created "by God," truly meets God. This divine intention was fully realized in the "Son of man," the person who was also the Son of God. Through participation in the life of Christ, we become "children of God," truly united with God and simultaneously truly human.

Jesus Christ exists in us. He comes to us through faith, through baptism, through the Eucharist. Through baptism, Christ comes once and forever. Through faith and the Eucharist, he comes always anew. Moreover, Christ comes always anew through the raising up of one's heart to God, through prayer and obedience, through all that divine providence sets as one's challenge and as one's destiny. Thus God lives in the Christian. To be more precise—and this is not a presumption as we speak in this way but a petition and a hope—God lives in me as that effective power, as that inspiration who wills to grasp my entire being so that I should be transformed "to resemble Christ," to live in "the fullness of Christ," and hence to Christian maturity.

God abides in me with saving power, as the One who has endured sin, suffered through death, and has risen to new life. God gives me a share in this saving power. When I, believing and trusting, live as God wills, then "it is no longer I who live, but it is Christ who lives in me" (Gal. 2:20). God is in me with the radiance of divine holiness. This holiness penetrates my heart and my will. It is enters into the inner realm of my freedom so that from there it can influence my entire being.

All of this is God's living in us. First, Christ is the "child" in the believer; he is undeveloped, incipient. Then Christ awakens in the person, and the stages of maturing occur: questioning, coming to an inner enlightenment, acting, and suffering. The person may eventually reach the fullness of old age and proceed through suffering to glory. —CI, 139–40, 143–44

THE DARKNESS AND LIGHT OF GOD (1936)

God is distant from us because God is the Lord of creation and the judge of sinners. God exists independently from us and is not reachable by us solely on the basis of our own experience or thought. At the same time, God is near to us because, out of his holy freedom, God comes to us and abides with us. While we cannot know God only on the basis of this world and human life, we can know God because of divine revelation, and what we learn is that God has become human.

God's "humanity" is proclaimed in the New Testament. Through faith, we realize that God is not the philosopher's "absolute being," but something else. Also through faith, we are aware that, through the gift of grace, a human being is neither only a natural being nor only a cultural being — which are notions prevalent in the sciences and in popular consciousness — but something else.

This mystery of "God with us" determines the Christian perspective on life, and it is expressed in authentic Christian teaching.

The Lord's Prayer reveals how this Christian sense of God's nearness expresses itself in prayer, which is conversation directly with God. The Lord's Prayer — as well as the Sermon on the Mount and the parables of Jesus — are the purest and ultimate testimonies to the mystery of God's nearness to us.

God, the unknown One, is in fact the known One. I do not apprehend God, and nevertheless I know God well. God conceals himself; however, God also discloses himself. Thomas Aquinas said, "Although on our own we do not know who God is, we know God as the One who comes here from afar." As the One coming out of mystery, God is the soul's ultimate happiness.

St. Paul makes a puzzling statement when he says, God "dwells in unapproachable light, whom no one has ever seen or can see" (1 Tim. 6:16). No one can ever see this light. It is beyond our perception. Beyond our perception, too, is the One from whom the rays of light stream. Does this mean then "darkness"? Why doesn't St. Paul say that God dwells in darkness? This is correct: it is a "darkness," which is simultaneously a light. And, although we cannot perceive this light, we can nevertheless have confidence in God.

Here is a knowledge that is not knowledge. A nearness that seems distant. A presence that is an absence.... We sense that all of this must be so because God is God. God enters into everything. With tender, yet powerful energy, God comes to us. This is the vitality of God. —ZKG, 402, 407–8

DIVINE PROVIDENCE (1936)

A message recurs in the New Testament. It is that Christ has revealed God's providence to us. Many parables speak of this: the one about the sparrow that does not fall from the roof without God knowing it; the one about the birds whom God nurses, and the one about the flowers which God clothes. We are admonished not to be anxious about food and clothing, but to petition God for bread for today and tomorrow, trusting that the future rests in the Father's hands. And there always resounds the mystery of the intimate words: "Your heavenly Father knows that you need all these things" (Matt. 6:32).

Time and again, this is the message: In your being and in your life and in all that matters, you are surrounded by an infinite goodness. What occurs does not come about by chance, but works for your good because a divine, loving concern for you guides the course of events in your life.

"Providence" — literally "looking for" — means that in everything that occurs there is a "looking out for," and what is looked out for is me. God's providence is working for what is good for me. God sees all that happens in the world and is attentive to everything. God notices all that harms me and all that is helpful to me. "No hair falls from my head" without it being noticed and considered in relation to my well-being. There is at work in world history an intention, a heart, a concern, and a power that is stronger than all worldly powers. This power brings about what the divine heart intends and what the divine intention wills. —VLG, ch. 2, pp. 25, 27–28

REFLECTIONS ON THE MYSTERY OF GOD (1937)

The God whom Jesus proclaimed is the One who asks for my love and makes me somehow capable of loving God as though I were equal to God. I receive from God the "permission," that is, the appropriateness of my loving God in this way, and this appropriateness is itself divine love.... As this love matures in me, it prompts me to say: I love God because God is God. I love God because it is right that God exists. All that I do should affirm God's existence because God is worthy "to receive power and wealth and wisdom and might and honor and glory and blessing" (Rev. 5:12). —HE, pt. 2, ch. 2, pp. 99–100

When believers get concerned about preserving pure doctrines and when there exists a religious body which speaks on behalf of these doctrines, there arises the danger of "orthodoxy." This so-called orthodoxy upholds the true doctrines as salvific in themselves, and, in their defense of purity of doctrine, ecclesiastical authorities harm the value of conscience. When there are fixed religious rules, rituals, and communal regulations, there arises the danger of regarding their exact execution as itself salvific. When there exists a hierarchy of offices and authorities, of traditions and laws, there arises the danger of seeing God's kingdom as already realized in human authorities and in obedience to these authorities. When there are established norms with regard to what is sacred and when there are distinctions about what is right and not right in religious matters, there arises the danger of human hands trying to control God's freedom. There is also the danger of trying to capture in rules what can come only from God's grace. An intention may be noble, but as soon as it enters into the realm of human life, it can result in just the opposite of what is intended, in lack of truth and in evil. A similar kind of distortion happens when God's revelation comes to expression in human forms. —HE, pt. 3, ch. 3, p. 198

Who is the God of Jesus? If God has revealed God's self in the person of Jesus, in the destiny of Jesus, then God must be the same as Jesus. What becomes manifest in Jesus about God? . . . Is it not revealed that God not only fulfills us, inspires us, and deeply affects us, but that God has "become" one of us (John 1:11)? . . . What Jesus did, God does. What Jesus endured, God endures. God does not step away from anything in human life.
—HE, pt. 5, ch. 3, p. 391

God is Spirit. "Spirit" means here not "mind," "logic," or "will," but "Holy Spirit," *pneuma. Pneuma* is that pure openness of being and at the same time the sure freedom of the divine person who is capable of fully realized love: the unrestrained uniting in one genuine self of I and you. That God lives in this clear personal differentiation and essential community is possible because God is "Holy Spirit." In the third person, in the Spirit, exist the Father and the Son, who are entirely open to each other, and simultaneously each is a distinct person. . . .

To be a true neighbor means to overcome the exclusivity of "me not you," of "mine not yours," and to overcome it without the destructive interaction in which personal boundaries get blurred and the dignity of each person is overshadowed. To be neighbor means not an accomplishment that is possible by human energy and perception, rather it is something new that comes from God; it surpasses the logic of mere differentiation and union. It is a new possibility of human existence, namely, the love of the Holy Spirit between people. Christian love does not mean that the I and the you are bound together by a fusing of the two individuals or by a loss of one's self. Instead, it means openness to the other and simultaneously personal individuation, communion, and individual dignity as they come through the Holy Spirit. —HE, pt. 5, ch. 6, 528, 530

TRUTH (1945)

Truth is a power especially when we require of it no immediate effect, but have patience and figure on a long wait. Still better, truth is a power when we do not think in general about its effects but seek to present it for its own sake, for its holy, divine greatness.... As already said, we must have patience. Here months may mean nothing and also years. Further, we must have no specific aims. Lack of an agenda somehow sets free the greatest power. Sometimes, especially in recent years, I had the sense that truth was standing as a reality in the room.

BML, 109–10

GOD'S DISTANCE AND NEARNESS (1952)

The mystery of God's distance and nearness repeats itself in the experience of each of us. Everyone knows how wonderful it is when God is near, and how difficult it is when God is distant. One cannot say what occurs on the other side in God. Even when all seems empty, and when our soul has difficulty uttering the words of a prayer, God is there. We exist only because God is there. Accounts of the life of the Egyptian desert hermit

St. Anthony tell how someone — after enduring God's distance for a long time — asked, "Lord, where were you during this terrifying time?" And God answered, "Nearer to you than my distance from you!"

God is always near, existing at the origins of our existence, speaking in the depths of our conscience. Nevertheless, it is evident that we experience our relationship with God between the poles of distance and nearness. Through the nearness, we are strengthened; through the distance, we are tested. When God allows us to feel his presence, his nearness, it is easy for us to be faithful to God. However, when God is distant from us, then there comes a period of naked faith that has nothing to hold on to other than the words, "I will not leave you" (John 14:18).

— MEN, 75–76

From his seventy-fifth birthday in 1960 until his death in 1968, Guardini frequently reflected on the incomprehensibility of God and asked about suffering and evil in the world.

A LETTER ABOUT GOD (1963)

My dear friend, I wish to share with you in a series of letters what, I judge, is the conclusion to my life's work. If it seems warranted, you may eventually make these letters public. In any case, I would like to give answers here to questions that I have pondered for a long time. As I do so, I must remind myself that every theological statement is only a partial expression of an aspect of the mystery of God.

In this first letter, I would like to undertake an inquiry that tries to penetrate so deeply into God's inner life that it may violate the appropriate reverence due to God. But my intention is noble. I would like to shed light on God's faithfulness, which surpasses all our thoughts, as does God's generosity. In this reflection, I would also like to explore that aspect of the divine mystery that is usually referred to with the frequently misused word "love." If my thoughts are correct and contemplated with one's mind and heart, they will lead to prayer. It is not God's power, but God's gracious orientation toward us that moves men and women to surrender to God in loving worship.

An important and decisive question at the outset of a theological inquiry may be posed: what is the motive behind this investigation? In general, such an inquiry is pursued out of a concern for salvation. I do not need to argue for the appropriateness of this motive. But is this intention ultimately decisive? Should not theologians be concerned above all about God? Shouldn't they rightly feel that they must stand in faithful awareness before the whole grandeur of God's glory? And shouldn't this motive warrant a theological inquiry?

For a long time some interconnected ideas have unsettled me, and in recent months they have urgently come to my consciousness. Strangely enough, these ideas came to me while I was reading the memoirs of C. G. Jung. (Jung's thought has led to some errors in theology.) In religious questions, the word "problem" frequently turns up in discussions about God: whether God is, how God is known, how God must be thought about, and whether life can be better lived without God. These issues and others like them lead to misunderstandings that open one's eyes to the fact that the appropriate way of thinking about the relationship between God and human beings has been destroyed. It seems to me that here is situated the dilemma of human beings, of the finite world. Is it not "enough" that God is? Can the finite exist "beside" God when God is indeed "God" and God alone? Human beings in search of God believe that they have met all of the conditions for knowing God when they acknowledge that God exists. But the unapprehendable character, indeed "incomprehensibility," of God's truth, of God's "honor," means that there always exists "something" in God that human beings have not thought about. (It is out of a recognition of the divine mystery that I put some words in quotation marks.) God's incomprehensibility has always made me restless to know more about God.

God simply is. The verse in the book of Exodus from which all thought about God proceeds and which is always in need of further clarification runs: "God said to Moses, 'I am, who I am.' He said further, 'Thus you shall say to the Israelites, I am has sent me to you' " (Exod. 3:14).

God simply is the essence, the power, the value, and the meaning of existence. God is existence, holy existence, which purely exists from God. God is sufficient in God's self, always moving and yet complete. What can it mean therefore for God when God creates the finite world which — since it moves toward us — reaches its high point in human beings?

In response to this question, one may immediately think about the "motive" behind the finite world, our world, and may say, "God's goodness has moved God to create the world and to call human beings into existence so that they should have the good fortune of personal existence and the possibility of eternal life." —TBF, 7–9

THE GOD OF THE BIBLE (1963)

The One to whom the psalmists pray is the living God who transcends the entire world. We cannot here answer the difficult question about the truth concerning the "gods." To simplify things, we shall speak about the gods as though they are real. In any case, they are dependent on the world. Zeus exists only because there is the vault of the heavens and the order of the constellations. Gaia exists because there are the dark and fruitful depths of the earth. By contrast, the God of the psalms has no need of the world. God exists in God's self and through God's self. At the decisive moment on Mount Horeb, God revealed himself as "Yahweh" (Exod. 3), the name that in all languages is represented by the title "Lord." God is "the Lord" not just because God governs the world, but because God is sovereign in God's very self.

This God is the One to whom the psalmists pray. This God frees all those who believe in the Lord from the manipulation that occurs in every form of pagan religion, even when this religion is quite noble. The Lord lifts those who call upon him to a freedom that human beings cannot find in this world, not even in the boldest metaphysics nor in the most profound wisdom.

We are taught that God has a name. God himself revealed this name on Mount Horeb. It is "I am" (Exod. 3:14). This name brings to mind a Hasidic story. After a rabbinical student finished his studies, he left his teacher and embarked on his own life. Then one day he decided to visit his former teacher. He reached his house at night and knocked on the closed door. From within, the teacher asked, "Who is there?" The student replied, "I am." There was a long silence. Finally the teacher said with great seriousness, "Who may say 'I am' except the Holy One, God?"

Human beings who know what they are doing cannot properly say "I am," or even "I am so-and-so"; they know that these words belong to God alone. To be is God's nature, and God's name is God himself in the form of two words. All people should praise God because God has given them their very existence. —WP, ch. 1, p. 124; ch. 6, p. 178

GOD'S WISDOM (1963)

When God created the world, God did not create as we might, making something in order to boast of it or to suit our own needs. God created the world out of pure — if we may use "pure" in its highest sense — joy, out of divine delight. God has created everything so that it may exist and so that it may be truthful, genuine, and beautiful. God's freedom and joyfulness in divine creative activity surpass our understanding.

How are we to understand God's guidance of the world? What does "providence" mean? Doesn't God have divine intentions for us? Doesn't God lead every human being and all of history to the goal that God has in mind? Isn't the life of each person ordered as it is because this person is connected with other persons in a definite manner? Are not the lives of all human beings ordered toward others, and all of created existence influenced by divine wisdom? Again we must differentiate among the meanings of the words that we use. What divine wisdom desires is not that God's intentions for us are somehow external or secondary to our intentions for ourselves, but that God's intentions are our intentions, our truth and our fulfillment.

This shared intending is the power that unites one thing with another, that draws one event into relation with others, and brings one human being into solidarity with other human beings, and all people into communion with one another. This divine guidance is not simply an "intention" but "wisdom." It is the sovereign wisdom of the perfect teacher who creates human existence as a tapestry in which every thread supports other threads and is simultaneously supported by them. However, we are not yet able to see the design of this tapestry. At this time we can perceive the tapestry only from its backside, and we can follow only short stretches of individual lines, then we lose track of them. But this tapestry will eventually be turned around —

at the end of time, in the final judgment. At that moment the tapestry's great patterns will clearly stand out. Then, too, we shall hear answers to our questions that received only partial answers or perhaps no answers during our lives, questions such as: Why? Why these hardships? Why these deprivations? Why did this occur and not that? All of the questions raised by life's injustices will be answered by divine wisdom — the wisdom that will have brought it about that the people and events of our lives did not simply occur by chance but have formed a coherent whole, a "world." — TU, ch. 8, pp. 80–81

GOD'S GOODNESS (1963)

If we could glimpse God's goodness, this endless wealth of good intentions, we would be joyful throughout our lives. That the world even exists is itself a permanent effect of God's goodness. The world would not even exist if God did not desire it. God does not need the world. Why should the infinite God need the world? God created the world and has sustained it because God is good. Someone may ask, however, does the world look as though God cares for it? Does human life appear to be the fruit of divine goodness? An honest answer is, Certainly not! Time and time again, men and women find themselves asking God, why are things as they are if you are good? This question is truthful as it arises in our burdened hearts. At the same time, however, this question is foolish in itself. What is the source of all the misery that makes life hard for men and women? Human beings themselves have brought about this misery.

The complaint arises, how can God be good? How can God be good when everything is as it is? But this question is usually asked with little thought about the origins of evil. God originally gave the world into human hands so that men and women could build up creation by cooperating with its creator. The book of Genesis presents creation as a paradise which human beings did not want. We wanted not God's kingdom but our own kingdom. Because of this rejection of God's offer, there has come about confusion, falsehood, and destruction in human activities. How can we get upset and declare, "God, if you were truly good, you would not have created such a world"? Yet the destruction of creation by human beings continues — by us who have made accusations against God.

The fact of the matter is that each of us can make life worse piece by piece. Every nasty word that we utter poisons the atmosphere. Every lie and every violent act have an impact on human existence and put us deeper into confusion. We have made our lives into what they are. It is dishonest, therefore, when we stand up and declare that God could not be good when our situation is what it is. Rather we should say, "Lord, give me the patience to endure what we have brought about. Give me also the will to do something to improve the situation in which I now find myself." This is the only honest thing to say.

But someone could interject something else, that is, the question of how God could be good when those creatures that could not be evil, namely, the animals, experience so much suffering. Many earnest people have made no headway in answering this question. How can God's goodness be present in the world when innocent creatures continually suffer so frightfully? I will be straightforward: I have no answer to this question.

One thought has, however, helped me that perhaps can help other people, namely, the sense of what "good" means when it is used in reference to God. We have the right — and even the obligation — to form concepts on the basis of glimpsing

God's character in creation and in our own lives so that we can try to understand God. Thus we can say God is just, God has patience, God is good, and so forth. These are important statements with which we can take concepts derived from creation's majesty and beauty, purify them of their inadequacies, and then apply them to God, the creator.

But this matter requires more thought. We know what the word "just" means when it is applied to human beings because we are finite beings and able to understand ourselves by means of finite concepts. But what happens when we use the word "just" in reference to God, who exists beyond all of our calculations and concepts? Do we comprehend what "just" means in talk about God, or does its meaning slip in a sense from our hands?

This much should be said here concerning our thinking and speaking about God: all finite beings have received their very being from God. Thus we can take one of the traits or qualities of our existence, put it into words, and use these words in relation to God. We can appropriately say, God possesses this property or quality but in an entirely perfect manner. God has the ideal of this property, which is found in a derivative and finite form in creation. In other words, when our words refer to God, their meaning eventually disappears in the mystery of God, and we can do nothing other than stand in awe before God's majesty.

In light of this reflection, let us return to our reflection on God's goodness. If I am speaking about a mother, for example, and say that she is good and that her whole family experiences her goodness, I know what my sentences mean. Indeed, I can express no more beautiful truth about someone. But what happens when I say that God is good? I initially know what my statement means. But as I think about what I've said, I sense that the mystery of God takes my words and pulls them away from my control. The direction of my word becomes like the bright trail that a meteor makes as it disappears into the unfathomableness of outer space. There remains a stillness which conveys a sense of my words' direction, and there arises an awe that marvels before the divine mystery. All of this leads to adoration.

To answer then the question posed at the outset: God is good even in those situations where we cannot make sense of God's goodness. —TU, ch. 11, pp. 106–8

A PRAYER TO THE LIVING GOD (1948)

Lord, living God, you are the One and the Only, and there is no other beside you. All divinity is yours, and whatever is not properly attributed to you is a theft.

In grace you have revealed your being to us and told us your name. We believe in you. Keep us in this faith, O Lord, for in it alone are we sustained. Your honor is our honor, and your governance is our salvation.

You have created the world and us in it. Everything—being and existence, life and meaning—comes from your omnipotent and loving word. And so we bow down before you, O Lord, and pray to you.

You are the Holy One. We are however sinful and acknowledge this. We are grateful to you for showing us our sinful condition since this is the truth, and only truth makes it possible for us to begin anew and to overcome our sinfulness.

You, O God, are the Lord. You are Lord in yourself, in your being for all eternity. You revealed yourself to your messenger Moses when you said to him: "I am who I am" (Exod. 3:14). You are also Lord of the world; you created it and govern it. At the same time, you respect the freedom of your creation, and give it the space to desire and to decide for itself. Grant that I do not forget you and do not misuse your generosity. Holy and gracious God, Lord of our lives, preserve me from that!

I pray to you, O God, for you alone "are worthy to receive glory and honor and power" (Rev. 4:11). Amen.

—TG, ch. 3, pp. 10–11

Chapter 3

Christian Faith

O Lord, you have searched me and known me.
—Psalm 139:1

Is belief in Jesus Christ no different from belief in Santa Claus, the Easter bunny, and the tooth fairy? Should we outgrow Christian faith just as we moved beyond our childhood fantasies? Authentic Christian faith is not trust in an imaginary being, nor is it a blanket under which to hide during stormy days and dark nights. According to Romano Guardini, belief in Jesus Christ directs one's whole self to the heart of reality. It engages our minds and our hearts in a new way of seeing and in relating to God, others, and self. It gives us the insight and strength to enter fully into life.

Guardini himself experienced a crisis of faith when he was twenty years old. This turning point in his life led to his recognition that Christian belief consists of more than a knowledge of the church's teachings. It is self-involving, and it requires one's participation in the believing community, even amid the flaws in the church as an institution. In his last years, Guardini acknowledged that a mature Christian faith even includes moments of doubt about God and Jesus Christ.

LOSING ONE'S LIFE (1945)

I went through a significant change in 1905. What had led me away from faith were not genuine reasons against it, but the fact that the reasons for faith were no longer clear to me. Faith as a conscious act had become increasingly weaker and finally had died. Nevertheless, I think that my unconscious relationship to Christ was never entirely sundered. It was important, too, that I had no complaint against the church or against a church official, and that the needs of my anxious conscience, which was closely tied to the church, had not brought me into conflict with the church. Now the religious desire came strongly from within me. This immediately led, as things unfolded, to a closeness to Christian faith.

What considerations affected me, I can no longer say in detail. An awareness has come about that justified and formed the whole inner event, and has remained for me since then the proper key to faith. I remember the very moment, as though it were yesterday, when this awareness led to a decision. I was in the attic room of my parents' house on Gonsenheimer Street in Mainz. My friend Karl Neundörfer and I had just discussed the issue of faith that concerned both of us, and my last words were, "It will come out of the verse: 'Whoever clings to his life will lose it; whoever gives his life will find it.' " My interpretation of Matthew 10:39 explains why this verse struck me. It had become clear to me that a law exists whereby a human being, if he "holds on to his soul" — which means if he remains in himself and considers as important only what enlightens him — loses his individuality. If he wants to find the truth and to attain his true self in the truth, then he must let go of himself. This insight surely had some preparatory steps, but I can no longer recall what they were.

After my last words, Karl Neundörfer went into an adjacent room that led out to a balcony. I sat at my desk, and I thought,

"Let go of my soul—but to whom? Who is in a position to ask this of me? To ask it so that I do not take it back again? Not simply 'God,' for when we have only to do with God, then we say God and mean ourselves. There must be an objective reality that can draw me out of every hiding place for self-control. There is only one such object: the Catholic Church in its authority and exactness. The question of holding on to or letting go of my soul would be decided ultimately not in relation to God but in relation to the church." This insight came to me as though I were holding everything—really "everything," my very being—in my hands. It was as though I were standing before a scale on which rested equal weights, and I were saying, "I can allow the scale to sink to the right or to the left. I can surrender my soul, or I can hang on to it." And then I let the scale tilt to the right, to the act of surrendering my life to God. At that moment everything became completely still. There was not a shaking, nor a flash of light, nor some kind of event. There was the entirely clear insight: "So it is." And the imperceptible, gentle sequel, "So it will be!"

Then I went to my friend, Karl, and told him what had occurred. Something similar had in fact taken place in him. He was struck by the words, "The greatest likelihood for discovering the truth happens where there is the greatest possibility for love." These words prepared him for the overcoming of his natural inclination to demand precision and correctness and also to be certain and fully aware of things. He acknowledged that he lacked the world of love, and the fullness of life depended on attaining it. Thus for him the question had concerned where he would find the way to love, and he had received the answer: through the church.

During the following days, I was very happy, with a peaceful and calm happiness.

My lectures at the University of Berlin from 1923 to 1939 were attended not only by students but also by people from various walks of life. Some were professors from the university's different faculties. Among them were some who had a short-lived curiosity in what I had to say. But many professors had a genuine interest in the subject matter of my lectures. Doctors, lawyers, and other professionals also came to my lectures. Now and then, there appeared a colleague who simply wanted to listen to me, to this "unusual lecturer." The students who were members of the Catholic youth movement were recognizable by their very spiritual presence. The students who were members of the official Catholic student associations usually took little or no interest in my lectures, unless they were also active in the Catholic youth movement. This lack of interest was a sign that many of the Catholic students were not religiously and spiritually engaged in a pursuit of the truth. Their religious ideals fit with their concern for wearing the right clothes and for pursuing their careers. The official members of the Catholic academic community ignored my lectures. From the outset, I was also denied every form of official ecclesiastical support. For this reason, I was free from oversight by church authorities.

During the decisive period of my life from 1918 to 1922, I realized that bishops and priests are not meant to control spiritual matters; they should not force believers to struggle to find a place in the church. If I had not come to this insight, I would have left the church and gone on my own way. I perceived that the church embodies the essential third element, the Holy Spirit, in the process of revelation. The Lord said, "No one knows the Father except the Son and anyone to whom the Son chooses to reveal him" (Matt. 11:27). The Son, Christ, no longer exists, however, in a historical space, but has sent the Holy Spirit to lead us "into all truth" (John 16:13). This is so essential that, according to the apostle, we are not able to say " 'Jesus is Lord' except by the Holy Spirit" (1 Cor. 12:3). The Spirit acts among us not as a wildly surging spiritual force, but in relation to a historical reality, namely, the church. This is the process of revelation: a person comes to the Father through the Son, and one sees Christ properly only in the church, which is guided by the Holy Spirit. How then can someone who is intent on discovering the truth about human life try to do this as a private endeavor? Wouldn't this approach be laughable? Those who seek the truth must welcome the church as much as possible into their lives. It was not therefore an accident that the first book in which I addressed the issues of our day was *The Spirit of the Liturgy* (1918), which developed the idea of the objectively ordered life of worship in the church. My second publication was *The Church and the Catholic* (1922), which begins with this sentence: "A religious process of unforeseeable significance has commenced: the church is awaking in the souls of all believers."

The church is surely not identical with the hierarchy, a theological school, or a traditional form. It is more than each of these parts, and each discrete part is meant to provide access to the church's totality and its essence. I know that this idea must be asserted and pursued with caution, for authority becomes actual in a specific situation, and obedience must be undertaken in relation to this situation. Nevertheless, there exists in each believer an immediate relationship with the church in the fullness of its essence, and on the basis of this relationship it is possible to go one's own way "in confidence," as St. Paul said, when personal insight and one's inner self demand it. I must add that I was devoted to the church even when I went down my own path to serve it.

The issue of Christian consciousness has fully engaged me over the years. I do not mean that I have concerned myself simply with the Christian faith. We become faithful at the moment we acknowledge God's revelation and seek to obey its word. As I understand it, Christian consciousness means that the fact of divine revelation becomes one's starting point and the spiritual order of revelation becomes one's way of thinking. It was for this outlook that I have struggled. I was convinced that within this orientation one could also attain a full view of the world and the important things of life. I have never viewed dogma as a barrier but as the system of coordinates for my thinking. I cannot say that I have fully realized that which I have mentioned here, but this was the goal that I never questioned.

My approach has not permitted me to work on conventional theological topics. When it was necessary, I have made myself do this, and without much fuss. But on these occasions my creativity remained constrained. Thus I have always struggled for freedom — which often meant standing alone, being perplexed, and in conflict with others. Nevertheless, I was certain in this way to work not on the basis of my subjective interests but in relation to the great interconnectedness of the church. It appears to me that my life's journey has confirmed that my instincts were correct. My inner drive and my outer circumstances have converged with a precise coincidence that is astounding.

In this perspective, something comes into focus that fills me with great gratitude: the laity immediately accepted my writings in the 1920s and have continued to do so with increasing enthusiasm. In recent years, church officials have begun to show confidence in me. I welcome this ecclesiastical trust as a confirmation that makes me happy, and I hope that it will remain with me until the end of my life.

BML, 70–72, 44, 117–19, 44

Guardini's pastoral ministry among youth made him aware that many of them struggled — as he did — to retain and strengthen their Christian belief and also to remain in the institutional church. He honestly addressed their concerns in many of his writings.

FAITH AND THE CHURCH (1922)

Being Catholic means to affirm the church as it is, including its tragic aspects. This act originates for Catholic Christians out of their underlying affirmation of all of reality. They cannot withdraw into the realm of pure ideas, feelings, and personal experiences. If they were to withdraw, they would no longer need to make "compromises" because they would neglect reality itself and hence distance themselves from God. Catholics frequently must hear the reproach that they have tied the true Christian belief of the Gospels to worldly power and a human organization, that they have made this belief into a religion of Roman laws, a religion of worldly goals, and have lowered Christ's high ideals to short cuts. This kind of criticism is expressed in a variety of ways. In fact, Catholics face the hard duty of reality. They would prefer to renounce the romanticism of ideals and experiences rather than to forget that Christ wanted his followers to bring all of reality into God's kingdom.

Here is an apparent paradox: ambiguity belongs to the very being of the earthly church as a historical reality. We may not disregard the visible church in favor of an ideal church. We can certainly assess the church's current condition in relation to what the church should be, and we can work to improve the church. This duty is placed upon priests at their ordination and upon lay people at their confirmations. But we must always affirm the actual church, place ourselves in it, and then proceed from this point.

This stance presupposes that we have the courage to live with continual dissatisfaction. The closer God is to us and the more important Christ and his kingdom become for us, the more we suffer from the church's inadequacies. This is the painful burden that weighs heavily on the souls of the great Christians, along with the joys of being children of God. Catholics cannot avoid this pain. They must prize not an aesthetic church, not a philosophical construct, not a community of a new age, but a church of human beings. This is a church that is divine and also human, spirit and flesh, indeed earth. This is the case because "the Word became flesh" (John 1:14), and the church is nothing other than Christ becoming and progressing into the proper communal substance and proper communal form. We live with Christ's promise that the wheat will never be suffocated by the weeds.

Christ lives in the church, but he is Christ crucified. We would even dare to make the comparison that the church's inadequacies are Christ's cross. The whole reality of the mystical Christ — his truth, his holiness and grace, his person which is worthy of adoration — is nailed to this cross as Christ's body was nailed to the wooden cross. And whoever wants Christ must accept his cross. We cannot remove him from it.

—VSK, ch. 3, pp. 51–53

A PERSONAL COMMITMENT (1926)

What does it mean to believe in God? Not only that I accept the abstract claim that God exists. Surely I believe this. Faith is also, however, the movement of my very being toward God. In this act, I set myself close to God and bind myself to God in personal trust. But there is even more to faith. And in this is the saving kernel of faith: the risk, the gift, the "giving over of one's soul" to God. Living faith involves even more: an increasing consciousness of the sacredness of all reality. Cardinal John Henry Newman frequently used the word "to realize." We should express the truths of faith not only in words, and we should convey them not only in concepts. We should also acknowledge these truths by our personal commitment, realizing their content and their reality in our lives. We should elicit their power and their meaning so that we embody their content in ourselves, so that we give them real significance in the way we live; this is how we should believe in divine truths.

Wherever there is finite existence, there is a boundary, a limit. Wherever there is a specific reality, a specific form, and a specific identity, there is a boundary. At every point, at every sliver and moment of existence, there is a boundary. Yet at each boundary there is that which exists "outside," that which exists on the other side of the boundary, that transcendence which we can still know today. An earlier type of human perception viewed this "outside" as something still in the realm of the created world. But today we can acknowledge that the other side of the boundary is a transcendent reality. We encounter a boundary at every point of our existence. Whatever is definite is constituted by a boundary; it is entirely limited. And always the "other side" of this boundary — by which I mean not surroundings but the absolute — is a living, transcendent reality that we can experience. This is the realm of God. —EAN, 175, 179

THE LIFE OF FAITH (1935)

There are various roads to Christian faith. Which aspect of the Christian reality comes first or is experienced as the most important element varies. It may be Christ. The person who is searching for God may encounter Jesus Christ and experience him to be the one true, powerful, and sovereign reality. In this case, the believer then finds the Father by means of Christ's help and also comes to the church through Christ.... Or the starting point for faith may be the church because of its stability, the strength of its support, and the fullness of its teachings. All of these ecclesial traits point beyond the church to Christ.... Or, it may be that the living God, the Holy Spirit, breaks into one's consciousness, and it gradually becomes clear that truth and holiness can be found only in Christ's teachings, and that Christ speaks with unimpaired freedom only in the church.

There are no prescribed avenues to belief in God. God leads people as God wills. Moreover, God adapts to each individual. He appeals to a person's psychological characteristics and spiritual convictions. God is attentive to the time and place in which a person lives and also to the influences on the person's life. At work is always the guiding hand of divine providence.

The various roads to faith have, however, one common experience: a new reality arises before — or in, or over, or whatever preposition is most appropriate — the people who previously lived in themselves and their own world. This new reality breaks in from another realm. It comes from above, from the other side. This reality, this something, gets more compelling. It conveys power, truth, goodness, and holiness, and demands a commitment from each one whom God calls. The decision to welcome this strange, separate reality into the space of one's existence is difficult. It is hard to sacrifice one's self-sufficiency and self-determination. It means a disruption and a risk. Christ said, "Those who find their life will lose it, and those who lose their life for my sake will find it" (Matt. 10:39). This is the first loss of the soul. It involves acknowledging a second personal center, indeed acknowledging that this second center is the proper center of one's soul.

Now the struggle between the "two centers" begins. For a long time it can seem that these centers oppose each other, that the one seeks to deprive the other of life; each wants to draw to itself the person's heart, spirit, power, and blood. The unfolding of faith entails an interaction between these two centers. There occurs the reciprocal pushing, pulling, and backing off; also, there are conflicts and resolutions. The two sides eventually grow together and begin a Christian existence that can be expressed in St. Paul's words: "it is no longer I who live, but it is Christ who lives in me" (Gal. 2:20).

The possibility of further tension surely exists because God is always the Holy One, and I am a sinner. Christ is always the One "from above," the One who comes from the Father. He is never completely identical with what is human. By contrast, I am an individual who belongs to this world which has existed in rebellion against God since the first human being. Jesus Christ became a real unity of God and man. A human being is not God, and God is never solely a human being. Yet the essence of Christian existence lies in the fact that a human being exists in God and God in a human being so that the Christian exists in Christ. This is a unity whose depths cannot be expressed by means of a concept from natural human experience.

To what is Christian faith directed? It is oriented to the living God who has revealed himself in Christ. It is oriented however not to God "in general," vaguely intuited, or somehow experienced in human existence. Rather, Christian faith is directed to the One "who is the God and Father of Jesus Christ."

Who is this God?

God loves the world. He has created it and sustains it. He penetrates it, and all things exist in him. Yet God is not the world but exists independent from it, in the divine self.... Human beings come from God. They live in God and are real only insofar as they remain linked to God. But human beings are not God.... God speaks through all that exists. All creation proclaims God's honor. Yet God is different from all creation and exists in the mystery of unapproachable light, the One who is God.... God is near, indeed near to everyone. God abides in us, and we abide in God. Yet the distance from human beings to God is immeasurably great, indeed "absolute...." God is our source and the eternal locus of our being. God is our home and our destination. Yet God is foreign to us, so foreign that our hearts cower before God.

—VL, ch. 2, pp. 24, 26; ch. 3, pp. 31–32

FAITH IN JESUS CHRIST (1937)

We surely sense that it is different for us to work in the service of God than to work only for an earthly goal. The latter is determined by the decision to maintain oneself, by the pressure of producing, and by the wish to hold an office or to establish a career. The former—service of God—is determined by the desire to place every action at the disposal of God's design so that God can bring about the new creation.

—HE, pt. 3, ch. 6, p. 221

The life of faith involves the development of an awareness of reality. According to our usual perceptions—to be more precise, according to our confused perceptions—the body is more real than the soul, electricity is more real than thought, personal power is more real than love, necessity is more real than truth, and all of this together—which is the "world"—is more real than God. How difficult it is, even in prayer, to perceive that God is real. How difficult and rare is the gift of acknowledging that Christ is real, that Christ is truly more real and powerful than the material things of human existence. When this acknowledgment occurs, then a person can interact with others, join in daily activities, sense the powers of the surroundings and of the public realm, and still say that God is more real and that Christ is stronger than everything else. Who can say this? The life of faith, the work of faith, the exercise of faith—the daily exercise of faith when earnestly pursued—should create this kind of perception so that we perceive what is truly real.

—HE, pt. 3, ch. 8, pp. 234–35

Did the people who were living at the time of Jesus have an advantage over us? Was faith easier when Jesus walked in Galilee? Or at Pentecost, or in the cities when St. Paul spoke? Or at the time of the persecutions when the martyrs' courage shone forth? Or in the centuries of the great, medieval saints? Or today? Are one hundred years or five hundred years a significant difference for what's essential, for what comes from God? Faith entails grasping in spoken words and in historical forms what is being revealed and also what is being conveyed through the concealment of these words and forms. For the people at Jesus' time, the events must have been great because of their marvelous energy, and yet in the back of people's minds must have been the obstacle: who is this man? . . . The task of those who have come later is this: to hear the living Christ through the preaching, books, and examples, through the sacred actions of the Mass, through the church's artistic images, customs, usages, and symbols. This is difficult for us but apparently not more difficult than it was for the ancient people who perceived the Son of God in "the son of a carpenter." —HE, pt. 4, ch. 6, pp. 304–5

Faith means to see and to risk accepting that Christ is the truth. He is not only a teacher. If he were only a teacher, he would be the greatest teacher who existed according to universal standards of the truth. No, Christ is the truth itself (John 14:6). The truth of sacred reality begins with Christ. If Christ were to be annihilated, then the truth that he taught would no longer exist. Not only would the primary and best teacher of this truth disappear, but this truth itself would be eliminated. This living truth is Jesus Christ, the Logos. To believe means to accept Christ as the truth and to enter into his school.

Would someone believe correctly if he or she endorsed and upheld what Christ proclaimed? This would be a beginning. Faith entails entering into Christ's school with one's thought, with one's heart, with one's sense of right and wrong, with everything that constitutes one's human existence. We must consider that the entire ship of human endeavors is headed in the wrong direction. It does not help to go from one side of the ship to its other side or to replace one instrument with another. The whole endeavor must head in a different direction. Faith is therefore a process, an instruction, a formation in which our eyes are created anew, our ideas directed differently, and the norms themselves measured anew.

What does it mean, for example, that I exist? From a natural point of view, this is of course something given. From a philosophical perspective, it is a problem on which I can reflect. This reflection does not, however, bring about anything different. I remain myself and become even more of a puzzle to myself. How does my life appear from the perspective of faith? In faith, I see that I have been created. I learn that I am always receiving myself from God and hence existing in a mysterious relationship, being truly myself and simultaneously existing in God. I learn that I am unique and nevertheless God's creature; that I am free and yet living according to every principle of God's power.

Try to see yourself in this way. Keep trying, and your sense of your life will eventually change. You will see yourself in an entirely different way. What previously appeared to be obvious will become questionable. What you were once complacent about, you will now treat with reverence. What you once felt confident about, you will now approach with "fear and trembling." Where you formerly found yourself abandoned, you will now feel cherished and safe. You will exist as a child of the creator-God, and this relationship will make a difference to the very roots of your being. —HE, pt. 4, ch. 12, pp. 352–54

When we interact with the people with whom we are somehow associated, and when we simultaneously think about Christ, seek to understand Christ, and speak with Christ, then our interrelating with others is different than if we did not believe in

Christ. It is not that we have a mysterious power over them so that they overcome their personal weaknesses. Rather, it may happen that we gradually become more patient, more understanding, and more kind. We may also become more perceptive and less superficial in evaluating others. We may attain an ability to assess another's personal character. These traits are not of course unique to the Christian life. But they show how we change when we follow Christ.... Christians remain in their jobs in business, the postal service, and medicine, and they do the same things that non-Christians do. They do not necessarily use a machine more efficiently; they do not necessarily find it easier to make an accurate medical diagnosis. Nonetheless, when Christians do their jobs and simultaneously follow Christ, something is in fact different. Christians become more earnest and conscientious; they let go of what is false and see what is real.... The same occurs as Christians cope with the burdens and heartaches and needs of human existence. The stuff of life remains the same, but we as Christians relate to it differently. The difference is not easily named. Its manifestations are however clear: an illness is endured; an addiction is overcome; a hatred is set aside. In Christ, we see all things differently.

—HE, pt. 6, ch. 8, pp. 548–49

Beginning in the 1950s, Guardini reflected on Christian belief in the context of West Germany's secular society. He held that as Christians mature in their faith, they gain greater insight into themselves, others, and the quality of life around them.

OBEDIENCE TO GOD (1950)

Becoming a person is essential for full human existence. What this process involves can be clearly seen and affirmed by our moral judgments when our relationship to the living, personal God is deliberately determined by God's revelation, the revelation that we are God's children who are guided by divine providence. When we do not live in light of this divine revelation, then we may attain the consciousness of a highly commendable, distinguished creative person but not the consciousness of a truly authentic person, the consciousness of one who possesses a singular human identity beyond all psychological and cultural attributes. Knowledge of the true character of personal existence remains united with Christian faith.

Christian belief will continue to exist amid the dangers of our age, and it will stress complete faithfulness to God. Faith will involve total obedience to God since it concerns what is ultimate. Obedience is part of faith not because human beings are "heteronomous" — that is, inclined to obey human laws and human authorities — but because God is holy and absolute. Faith requires therefore an entirely unliberal attitude, namely, an unconditional orientation toward the unconditional One. But this orientation is undertaken in freedom, and it is this freedom that distinguishes obedience to God from obedience to human authorities. This unconditional act before God is not a surrender to the physical and psychological power of human commands. Instead, through this obedience to God, human beings accept by their actions the absolute uniqueness of God's demands. This act of obedience presupposes a person's maturity of judgment and freedom for making decisions.

Trust is a prerequisite here. Trust makes possible this obedience to God. This is not a trust in the general order of reason, or in an optimistic principle of good human intentions. It is a trust in God who is real and active in our lives.

—EN, ch. 3, pp. 86, 93

HOPE (1951)

Christian hope has a purely religious form and expresses itself in a person's trust that God is greater than all worldly processes. God has the world in his hand, and God's grace influences every human life in every age. God is intent not on the functioning of a machine but on the creation of a life-giving spirit.

There arises therefore the hope that God will inspire men and women not to be dominated by the technological and scientific powers that they possess, but to put them to good use, to exercise power not only over nature but also over their own human powers, and to direct these powers according to a proper sense of human life and human work.

There is now emerging the hope that there is coming a new type of human being who will not succumb to the dominating earthly powers but will be intent on controlling these powers. This new kind of man and woman will be equipped to exercise power not only over nature but also over power itself. They will subordinate the use of power to a respect for human life and human activity. —MA, ch. 4, pp. 167, 168

A DOUBTING FAITH (1961)

For a long time the Old Testament played no essential role in theology. It was seen primarily as a preparation for the New Testament. As a result, the Old Testament often became simply a subject within the general history of religion. In recent years a change has come about. It is becoming clear that the Old Testament has significance for understanding the New Testament, for example, for understanding the freedom of Christians in overcoming ancient myths, autonomous metaphysics, and long-standing forms of civil governance. This overcoming, which is a powerful process, is attested to in the Old Testament. Moreover, the Old Testament's teachings on creation — which tell of God's love for creation and which challenge believers to respect creation — play a decisive role in the deepening of the Christian relationship to the world. Much more could be said on this topic.

All of this goes together with what was previously expressed and has brought it about that Christians are taking a new interest in the religious meaning of the Old Testament. A concrete instance of this may be seen in the widespread high regard for the person and work of Martin Buber. Buber is not only a great man with a strong body of thought but also a spokesperson in European culture for the Jewish understanding of God and human life.

A new sense of things is arising: people are recognizing that they are responsible for the earth, indeed, that they must rescue it because every increase in scientific knowledge and technological power lessens the earth's stability, and because these advances in scientific and technological knowledge persistently continue at a greater and greater rate. Thus existence as a whole ends up in a heretofore unknown state of suspension: what seemed to make existence secure is revealed as that which now places existence actually and fundamentally in question.

The dangers of today's daunting scientific-technological culture challenge human beings in ways that are now evoking fresh elements of the Christian life, elements that were previously dormant. How this challenge will unfold and how Christians will interact with the anonymous impulses of the will to power, the drive for wealth, and the effort to do everything is a question that Christians have yet to answer. The ethical and pedagogical questions of power are still hardly even articulated. Nor is the question of a theology of power. To see power as simply evil is a great mistake — and a dangerous one in the present situation. According to the book of Genesis, human beings are made in the image of God. This resemblance includes the ability to govern the world. God is the Lord over creation because God is its creator. Human beings are God's creatures and govern by God's grace. Thus their governance is essentially bound to God's governance. Original sin is the outrage that attacks the fundamental relationship between God and human beings; it thus brings about the disorders that destroy the essence of human beings. This idea highlights the urgent need to think through anew the identity and mission of human beings in the world and to formulate their obligations to creation, obligations whose significance is not yet foreseen.

We must conclude that today's faith should arise out of an informed, reflective, self-critical assessment. A "doubting faith" must let go of many beautiful religious and liturgical expressions of faith in order to remain anchored in its essential elements. A faith that does not run from doubt — hence, a faith that remains authentic — does not distance itself from questions, but includes them. As Cardinal Newman has said, "faith is able to bear doubt." —MST, 278–79, 282, 283, 286

RELIGIOUS EXPERIENCE TODAY (1963)

The further we study history the more we see what "religious experience" entails. "Religious experience" means that sense that immediately feels or intuits a numinous element in all things, all occurrences, and all associations. It recognizes that all reality is more than that which today is widely called "empirical" experience. Reality is that which can be seen, measured, and comprehended, "plus" the fact that it is created by God and receives its existence from God. This religious perception of reality seems to grow increasingly weaker in our world.

Today's general crisis of faith exists to a large extent because of the decrease and perhaps disappearance of immediate religious experiences. One cause of this crisis is the total reliance on what people call rational inquiry and technology. Another cause is the fact that the created realm, that is, the world and human beings, are not seen in relation to God, but are "nakedly" perceived so that they become "merely" the world and "merely" human beings. The unnaturalness of this way of seeing the world and human life manifests itself in what philosophy, art, medicine, and psychology call the anxiety of contemporary human beings and their rootlessness, loneliness, and weariness.

This reflection prompts the question, how can contemporary human beings come to acknowledge God and have faith in God? Or, more specifically, what character will faith have if immediate religious experience really decreases, perhaps to the point that it disappears as a generally real factor? If the world receives increasingly greater significance as a reality on its own? If human beings attain increasingly greater power? If the appeal of the world overwhelms human beings? And if the world's challenges become increasingly more demanding and make greater claims on human beings?

It seems to me that the starting point for a person's acknowledgement of God must be an accurate and honest analysis of the finitude of the world and of human beings. By "honest" I mean that in the experience of finitude one must distinguish between the greatness of existence and the challenge of it, on the one hand, and the absoluteness of God, on the other. Hence, there should occur the awareness that a higher regard for the finite world, its reality, its value, and its challenges never results in something other than finitude. An intoxication with quantification must be seen for what it is, and people must admit that emptiness, anxiety, rootlessness, weariness are symptoms of the fact that contemporary human beings are focused only on what is finite. It must be shown that the human yearning for values and meaning seeks not only more and greater forms of finite reality but also the infinite, the absolute. It must be clear that this yearning for the infinite is not a flight from what is truly human, but is a categorical or actual expression of what is essentially human. This primary dynamism in human life can, in fact, be covered over by technology.

A further approach to religious experience is to gather imaginatively together moments when someone has sensed that something finite was in fact God's "work" and God's "image." While just one of these moments may not provide a basis for a person's belief in God, many of these moments can generate an acknowledgement of God. It seems to me that Cardinal Newman was correct when he observed that the real or actual basis for belief in God is not a simple syllogism but a cluster of concrete lines that converge at a point, and this "point" is God.

The starting point for a faith-guided understanding of the world is the incarnation. The Christian sees the incarnation of God not only as the revelation of salvation but also as the key for understanding existence in general. The Christian understands everything and its becoming, human history and its unfolding, as the expression of what we can call the history of God in his creation. In other words, the Christian understands the existence of all finite reality as a mystery in which God's unfathomable and sacred mind, the mystery of love, expresses itself. A Christian understands this love not in an anthropocentric sense but in its own theocentric sense. As a result, creation receives an objectivity and greatness so that it speaks more strongly to contemporary men and women than all pragmatic perceptions of creation. —TBF, 25–26, 27–28

ACTING WITH GOD (1963)

To believe means to be certain that God is acting since the beginning of creation until its end through the unfolding of all historical periods. To believe means doing what is demanded by the situation at the present moment and collaborating in the progress of God's actions toward the goal that God intends, namely, the second coming of Jesus Christ and the victory of God's kingdom. So we do well to break through the surface of a pure system of doctrines and to acknowledge that God is doing something even today, even here, even also with me. I must place myself in this convergence of things, and I must join in it, act in it, and fight for it. It is in this convergence that the meaning of "hope" will become significant and clear to me. That is, hope means having the confidence that Christ's good news will be realized despite everything that brings about the resistance of disbelief and disobedience and despite the apparent impossibility of the realization of the good news. Hope means trusting that the rebirth to new life will surely come about in me and in creation. —WP, ch. 12, pp. 225

A PRAYER FOR A LIVING FAITH (1948)

O God, the creator and Father of life, you have given us our lives so that we may live and grow and come to fulfillment. You have placed our lives in our hands so that we may live them properly, and you will eventually demand an accounting from us of what we have done with our lives.

At the same time, you have given us another life which awakens at the hour that your grace chooses in response to your self-revelation. This life originates in eternity. It is created by the Holy Spirit, the giver of life. You have also placed this spiritual life in our hands. We can preserve it in honor, or we can waste it. We can take care that this life grows and matures. Or we can neglect it and allow it to whither. And you will eventually demand an accounting of what we have done with our inner lives.

Let me always be aware, O Lord, that this spiritual life is within me. Strengthen me to care for this inner life, which is more real than my external life in the world. Allow me to sense how you cherish this inner life in which lies the ultimate meaning of my whole life.

Grant me a great commitment to everything that is important to believing in you. Teach me to recognize what faith needs in order to flourish and become fruitful. Make me trust this faith's strength and simultaneously know its weaknesses. And with the passing of the years, my ideas and feelings may bring about changes in the form of my faith, though not in its sacred content. If this occurs, teach me to understand these changes. Teach me, too, to stand firm amid the trials that may result from these changes so that my faith may grow and mature from one form to another, as you have desired. Amen. —TG, ch. 2, pp. 8–9

Chapter 4

Jesus Christ

The Lord is my shepherd, I shall not want.
—Psalm 23:1

Jesus Christ may seem at times to be solely a past figure, a man who was born two thousand years ago and died on a cross in Jerusalem. Or Jesus may appear to be primarily a teacher of morals. Facing a tough situation, we may ask: What would Jesus do? Yet he is more than these views express. As Romano Guardini explained, Jesus Christ is the mediator between God and creation. Christ unites God and us as he reveals the divine heart and simultaneously reveals and heals the human heart.

Guardini held that men and women are drawn to God by the Holy Spirit as they become united with the risen Christ. Christians have experiences similar to what happened to St. Paul on the road to Damascus (Acts 9). These religious moments generate various images and ideas of Christ and his significance for our lives. Amid this diversity of views, the constant factor is Jesus' suffering, death, and resurrection. Belief in the paschal mystery gives us hope that in union with Christ we shall join in the resurrection of the dead (1 Cor. 15:22).

MEETING THE RISEN CHRIST (1945)

My teaching at the University of Bonn lasted for only one year (1922–23), while I completed my second dissertation on St. Bonaventure's thought. During that time, I resided at Holtorf, which is a walk of two-and-a-half hours from Bonn; by train the trip is only thirty minutes. . . . I remember very clearly the origins of my essay "Gespräch vom Reichtum Christi" (A conversation about the Reign of Christ), which appeared in my small book *Auf dem Wege* (On the way) in 1923. I had been invited to the home of Bonn's art historian Paul Clemen (d. 1947) and had such a long, lively visit with him that I walked from Bonn to Holtorf at night. On the way home, there came to me an imaginary conversation that had no direct connection to my visit with Professor Clemen. In this conversation, three men take a walk together and discuss various aspects of the mystery of Christ, starting with the idea of the Sacred Heart of Jesus. While they are having this discussion, they realize that a fourth "person," Christ, has been walking behind them. When I arrived back at my residence, I immediately became engaged in the matters at hand. However, the entire complicated conversation remained in my mind. This occurrence indicates how my creativity bubbled up at that time, and also how little it was linked to normal theological scholarship.

—BML, 35

A CONVERSATION ABOUT CHRIST (1923)

I wish to begin by explaining why I have fashioned a theological text in the form of a conversation. The many diverse elements of a complex reality can be lost sight of in an account that is wholly conceptual. These various aspects can however come into view through an imaginative form of inquiry. This is especially the case when this presentation is a narrative with characters and events. The reflection that I have undertaken here is meant to make more visible the fullness of the figure of the God-man, Jesus Christ. The form of a conversation seemed most appropriate for this task. Here is an imaginary conversation about Christ.

The director of Catholic social services: Hello. I'm glad that I've bumped into both of you. May I walk with you?

The teacher: Surely. Our pastor has just pulled me away from my books. He is telling me about Hans, one of the young men in the parish. A couple of days ago, some thugs in the factory mistreated Hans because he disagreed with them when they were denouncing religion.... It sounds to me similar to scenes in the early church. As you tell it, Herr Pastor, the young man has witnessed to the risen Lord.

The priest: Yes, it seems similar to the time when St. Stephen was brought before the council in Jerusalem, and "his face was like the face of an angel" (Acts 6:15).... Such are our times! The Spirit groans! Norbert, an older man who also works in the factory, told me about the incident. It upset him just to recount what took place.... But enough for the moment about this incident. I sense that we should allow our friend from the Catholic social services to tell us what's on his mind. He seems preoccupied.

Director: I finished my work in the office and decided to head home. This morning I read a passage from the New Testament, and some biblical words have stayed with me all day. They are from the account in which the rich young man came to Jesus and asked: "Good master, what must I do to attain eternal life?" And the Lord responded almost harshly: "Why do you call me good? No one is good but God alone" (Luke 18:19). Does it strike you that Jesus' response is somewhat highhanded? I do not want to misread things, but this story has stayed with me all day. I keep trying to understand what it may mean. So I left my office and began to walk home with it on my mind. As I was passing St. Elizabeth's Church, I heard singing inside, and thought: "Why not go inside? It cannot hurt you after all of the hardship cases that you handled today." Inside, I found people engaged in the devotion to the Sacred Heart of Jesus.... Then the people sang a hymn with the words, "heart of Jesus, sweetest heart of Jesus." This hymn with its image of Jesus' heart upset me, and I left the church. Tell me, is this image of Jesus correct? Is this his identity?

Teacher: I have long thought about something that I think is now becoming clear to me. When I go to Mass or other forms of worship, I experience a strong religious burning within myself. This feeling can come about when one participates in the liturgy for Good Friday, or visits one of the new churches and sees how it expresses the spiritual world and how it rises and directs one's attention. A strong, surging sense can come about. Everything is illumined. The Logos lives here. Surely one does not find in worship, Herr Director, that earthly figure whom you seek, the figure with sharp individual characteristics. In worship, Jesus' human features are softened, presented on a higher level, and made sacred. So it is! Nothing of his humanity is denied, only transformed. Nothing is cut out, only clarified.

Director: The Christian faith is not a religion of ideas or of effective organizations, or of some kind of feelings and experiences — even though all of these elements are important. Christian belief is an entirely positive religion. It stands or falls with the historical person of Jesus. Christian belief is Jesus! We cannot experience who God is on our own. We can know that God exists, and that God is personal. But who God is, God's identity, we are not able to grasp by means of our speculation or intuition or spiritual experiences. Consider that we are not able to know another human being just by relying on our own ideas and experiences. We must see the other and speak with him or her, and then we can perceive and discern who and what he or she is. Something similar occurs in our knowledge of God. We can sense the absoluteness of God, the seal of God's infinite, invaluable singularity. But we cannot reason to God or make our way to God solely on the basis of our earthly existence. We are not able to see God, and we cannot go to God, because God "dwells in unapproachable light" (1 Tim. 6:16). However, we can acknowledge God, the living God, because God has come to us in an embodied reality, in Jesus. God "has become flesh," and has done so in the concrete person of Jesus, in the unique shape of Jesus' words and actions and self-giving. Here we see the identity of God. Jesus himself made this same point when Philip came to him and asked: "Lord, show us the Father, and we shall be at peace." Then Jesus said: "Philip, whoever sees me, sees the Father!" (John 14:8–9). Thus we can do nothing better than to stay with Jesus if we want to go to God. If we want to know God's ways, thoughts, and convictions, we must carefully notice and attend to Jesus' ways, thoughts and convictions. This is what it means to be Christian.

My ideas may seem strange to both of you. But think about them. What is Christian is the particular reality of Jesus, and in this reality the identity of God is revealed. It is the reality of this human being, the one "born of God." If we want to know what it is to be Christian, we must consider what Jesus thought about himself. Also, about the world, about the Christian life, and so forth.

Jesus is the way to the Father. We have nothing else to do but to stay close to Jesus. So we cannot ignore anything that he said and did and suffered; we cannot dismiss any aspect of his being. I would give everything if I could see Jesus, even for a moment! If I could see how he went across a street or how he turned to the sick, or if I could hear in what tone of voice he uttered a sentence.... Then I, too, would see God! Do you understand what I am saying?

Priest: Earlier today I visited the young worker, Hans, in the hospital. He is entirely wrapped in bandages, but he is doing better. I chatted with him about a number of things. Then I finally asked, "Tell me, Hans, why didn't you remain quiet when these crude men denounced religion?" He looked intently at me and said with great earnestness, "Recently at our meeting of Catholic young adults, some folks mentioned that it pains the heart of Jesus when people criticize religious belief. This idea prompted me to want to help Christ."

Aren't these extraordinary words? For my part, I am usually not comfortable with strong emotions. I felt very small beside Hans, despite all of my theology.

I have known Hans for a while, and he and I are at ease with each other. Since we had discussed religious matters before today, I eventually asked him, "Hans, do you still want to bring joy to the heart of Jesus?" He nodded yes. So I added, "Then bear your injuries bravely, and offer them to Jesus for the well-being of the thugs who beat you up. Can you do this?" He said nothing at this point, but I knew that he understood what I meant.

We must find a new word or expression for "truth" and "in love." St. Paul said that we must speak the truth in love (Eph. 4:15). Further, we know that "the Word became flesh" (John 1:14). We must not forget that these words mean "God is love" (1 John 4:8, 16), and hence love has become flesh. Jesus himself embodied this divine love. If he is a human being of this sort, then he is the savior through his words, his life, and his very being. Through him, the divine word burns and melts everything so that everything becomes more simple. Ultimately nothing remains leftover. There exists only a glowing ember in which everything is contained, and this ember is the heart of Jesus. When we grasp this reality, then we understand the Lord, what he is and all of his life and suffering and death. The believer's love is not the love found in this world. It is Christian love, the love possessed by God and Jesus. This divine love has descended among us and has become incarnate in Jesus, and it has burned until everything stood in flames. This is Christ, my friends!

When we have this reality in ourselves, then it is as though the whole world and our whole life is affected by Christ. Everything becomes very simple. Then our many motives are melted into one orientation: love of Christ. There is only one important consideration: God is love for me, and when I have this love, then I have God. When this occurs in a person of upright character, then great acts take place, as has come about in the noble heart of the young man Hans.

Director:... We have surely played out these views of Christ. My goodness! As we were speaking about Christ, we actually saw him.... Was this an illusion? What do you think?

Teacher: I believe that our time together has been blessed. Rays of light in pure differentiation have come upon us. The divine source — like the sun — that has sent these various rays is a unified whole. Yet we are human beings. Each one of us beholds Christ from a different standpoint, and each standpoint allows Christ to come into view for us. Although there are many standpoints, their object remains one and the same. This recognition of our differing perspectives demands that each of us remains humble and does not claim that the ray that appears bright to us is the fullness of the source. Each of us must acknowledge our limitedness and the source's radiating greatness. All people must open themselves to the whole truth and look beyond their limits. While people cannot apprehend the whole, the catholic or universal fullness of Christ, they must know nevertheless that this fullness exists, and they must remain in living unity with that which stands before them. Then there will grow in them the earthly figure presented in the Gospels, the eternal reality manifested in the liturgy, and the image of Jesus conveyed by devotions such as that to the Sacred Heart of Jesus. Surely people will continually observe the whole reality of Christ from their respective points of view, but they can remain conscious of his wholeness and maintain a living relationship with Christ.

—GRC, 259, 260–62, 263, 265–66, 268–69, 273

During his first years as a priest, Guardini became aware that while many people are faithful to the church's teachings, religious practices, and moral rules, they have not yet truly encountered the living Christ. For the remainder of his life, Guardini attempted to help people recognize Christ in their lives.

CHRIST IN THE GOSPELS AND IN THE LITURGY (1918)

Whoever wishes to apprehend the mystery of Christ in its whole breadth must notice how the figure of the Lord appears in the liturgy and the Gospels. In the Gospels, everything is related to a particular life. Readers breathe in the air of the Holy Land. They sense the era in which Jesus lived. They see Jesus of Nazareth in this world, walking on the roads and mixing with the people. They hear Jesus' unparalleled convincing words. They feel how these words flow from Jesus' heart and touch the hearts of his listeners. The attractiveness of historical reality permeates this image of the Lord. He is clearly one of us, a definite person, namely, Jesus, "the carpenter's son," who lived in Nazareth on a specific street, wore specific clothes, and spoke in a specific way. This view of Jesus appeals to modern men and women who rejoice in the fact that the eternal infinite God dwelt in a living, personal, and unified way in this historical figure, so that Jesus is in the fullest sense "truly God and truly a human being."

The figure of Jesus appears quite different in the liturgy. Here he is the majestic mediator between God and human beings; he is the eternal high priest, the divine teacher, the judge of the living and the dead. He is the one concealed in the sacraments, who in his body mysteriously unites all believers in the vibrant community of the church. He is the God-man, the word who has become flesh. Jesus' humanity, his human nature, is surely preserved; it remains certain. (In saying these words, one automatically turns to expressions found in the doctrine of God. The struggles against Eutyches are otherwise not resolved.) Jesus is truly, fully a human being, with body and soul, who really lived. He is, however, entirely transfigured and illumined in his divinity, raised into the light of eternity, removed beyond history, outside of space and time. He is the Lord who "sits at the right hand of the Father," the mystical Christ who now lives in his church.

—VG, ch. 3, pp. 44–45

THE LIVING CHRIST (1929)

Christian faith is primarily neither a doctrine nor a meaningful idea about life. It includes these, to be sure. But these are not its essence. Its essence is Jesus of Nazareth — his being, work, and destiny. In other words, the essence of Christian faith is an actual person. Anyone who is committed to another person experiences something similar to the Christian's relationship with Jesus Christ. In both cases, what is important is determined not by "humanity" in general or by "what is human," but by the man or woman to whom I am devoted. Moreover, the deeper and richer the other person, the more intense the relationship.

This relationship can become so powerful that everything — one's world, destiny, and task — is permeated by the beloved. He or she is somehow contained in everything and is signified by everything; indeed, the beloved gives meaning to everything. In the experience of great love, the world comes together in this intimate relationship, and all that happens becomes an event in this relationship.

This reflection has progressed far enough to yield an answer to the question of "the essence of Christian faith." It is that there is no abstract definition of this essence. There is no doctrine, no basic outline of ethical values, and no religious disposition or form of life that can be detached from the person of Christ and said to be the essence of Christian belief. What is essential to the Christian faith is Christ himself and that which comes through Christ to human beings and the relationship with God that a person can have through Christ.

A teaching is Christian insofar as it comes from the mouth of Christ. A life is Christian insofar as its movement is determined by Christ. In everything, what is Christian is that which Christ gives. The person of Jesus Christ in his historical uniqueness and eternal glory is himself the point of reference for the being, activities, and teachings of Christians. This is a paradox. . . . The Christian consciousness, the Christian act of confession and its method of development, and Christian theology must be approached so that Christ is the defining category of this consciousness and this confession. A consideration of these matters must occur so it does not seem to be a theoretical issue but a reflection on religious discipleship.

To bring this discussion to a conclusion, we can consider the assertion that Christian belief is the religion of love. This claim is correct when it presupposes that the love being considered here is properly seen. It is not love in general; it is not even religious love in general. The love spoken of here is that love which is related to a specific person, namely, Jesus Christ, who makes love in general possible. If we speak of Christian faith as the religion of love, then we must do so in a definite sense, namely, that it is the religion of love directed to Christ and through Christ to God as well as to other people. Further, it must be said that Christian faith entails not only a specific singular act but also "the first and great commandment," and on it "depend the law and the prophets" (Matt. 22:38). Hence, Christian faith is the absolute point of view. All aspects of life must be seen in relation to it. —WC, 14, 68–70

THE ONE WHO HAS PASSED THROUGH (1930)

"As long as I am in the world. . . . "
—John 9:5

The life of a human being is a web of events. Things and people — friendly and hostile, near and far — are part of this life. These influence, disturb, and challenge one's life. A person engages in the realities of the world: acting, creating, and experiencing a destiny. This whole multiplicity is connected with what we call the person's identity. In this whole, what has a special significance is the person's manner or way of being in the world.

We can differentiate among various modes of being in the world. A person may appear similar to a tree that grows up on valuable ground, quietly matures, realizes its potential, and then dies. This person is a stable presence in the world. . . . We may know another person who energetically pursues his or her career, assumes a role or position, works, struggles, and eventually accomplishes something — something that eventually comes to an end.... There is also the restless, searching person who is always on the go, living with risks and discoveries.... Moreover, there is the person of destiny who has strong ties with the deepest currents of human life; this one waits, encounters, awakens, brings about a breakthrough, perseveres, and endures.... And there are other ways of life as well.

Jesus' way of being in the world fits no type. When we read the Gospels, when we seek echoes of his life in the Acts of the Apostles and in the New Testament's letters, and then ask, how was he "there," we sense something singular, something that defies classification. We can perhaps express it best in the words: "He has passed through." Jesus' mode of life was a passing through. Although we know little about his life, we can glimpse his way of being in the world. At the end of his Gospel, St. John says that if all that Jesus did were written down, "the world itself could not contain the books that would be written" (John 21:25). The apostle John was conscious of the enormous richness of Jesus' very being. Behind every glimpse, behind every word and happening in Jesus' life existed an unending intensity and unfathomable depth. As a result, what was handed on about him is not much in relation to all that could have been said. When we pull together the reports of the Synoptic Gospels about what newness appeared in Jesus, when we take the singular testimony of St. John, and the little of what we find in the Acts of the Apostles, what comes together is really not very much! About the first years of his life, we hear a few events of his youth, then everything remains concealed in silence for eighteen years. By contrast, his public ministry stands in bright light. But it lasted only for three years, and it is not recounted at length. Then everything comes to an end. In other words, this life came out of silent incomprehensibility, briefly and powerfully shone forth, and then returned to incomprehensibility in "heaven."

Jesus himself spoke of his coming and going. "For that is what I came out to do," he said (Mark 1:38). He must not remain in one place but must also "go into the neighboring towns." According to Matthew, Jesus said three times: "I have come to . . . " (Matt. 10:34–35). This sense of movement occurs elsewhere, too.

Jesus' consciousness comes forth strongly in John's Gospel. Again, "I have come," and "A little while, and you will no longer see me" (John 16:16). "I go to prepare a place for you" (John 14:2). "Where I am going, you cannot come" (John 13:33).

The sense that he came, passed through, and then disappeared becomes still stronger when he says from where and to where, "from above," "from the Father," and again "to the Father," where "the eternal dwelling places" are. And, "I came from the Father and have come into the world" (John 16:28).

This inner orientation expressed itself in Jesus' day-to-day way of life. He lived as an itinerant teacher, which was not customary at that time. Lacking his own home, he went from place to place, taught, conversed with the people, and stayed where someone accepted him.

Jesus deeply and heavily felt this absence of a home. When the young man asked to be able to follow him, he answered, "Foxes have holes, and birds of the air have nests; but the Son of man has nowhere to lay his head" (Luke 9:58).

People warmly welcomed Jesus into their homes. We think above all of the household that he loved, that of Lazarus and his sisters in Bethany (John 11:1–3). We think, too, of the occasion when the Pharisee Simon invited Jesus into his home (Luke 7:36). At the same time, we sense danger gathering around Jesus. He was not welcomed; he was kept at a distance. When the woman came and wept at his feet, dried them with her hair, and anointed them with costly oil, a contemptuous disdain arose in Simon's heart: "If this man were a prophet, he would have known who and what kind of woman this is who is touching him—that she is a sinner" (Luke 7:39). Then Jesus turned to the host and said, "Simon, I have something to say to you....I entered your house; you gave me no water for my feet....You gave me no kiss....You did not anoint my head with oil" (Luke 7:40–46). This means that you have not fulfilled the most basic duties of hospitality. We would say that society did not accept Jesus. It is startling to read how those who were excluded from society extended this basic courtesy to Jesus.

The Lord's manner of life was that he "passed through." When we come close to someone, we glance at that person. We seek to grasp how the person appears, what he intends, his origins, and how he is viewed in the public arena. We seek to know him or her, not just externally, but also interiorly: who are you? Not only, what are you? With the what-question, I inquire into what I can expect from the person. But the deeper question is, who are you? With the who-question, I seek to know the person, to come interiorly to that person.

Thus we ask of the Lord, who are you? We do not know much when we know externally the words and the actions of Jesus. We do not know much when Jesus appears as that solemn, somewhat unreal, somewhat undefined figure with long hair and a pleated robe. All of this is a sketch. His essence must attain flesh and blood in our hearts. We must pursue him. We must look inquisitively at him. We must attempt to encounter Jesus in his uniqueness, to apprehend his very being. Then things come into view for us. —HG, 58–63

During the three hundred years prior to the Second Vatican Council, the celebration of Holy Thursday, Good Friday, and Easter Sunday was eclipsed in Catholicism by the church's many feasts and holy days. Guardini contributed to the church's refocusing on the central drama of Christian belief: Jesus' suffering, death, and resurrection.

JESUS' DEATH (1937)

Jesus Christ acted in love, in full awareness, with a free will and all his heart when he endured the free fall into nothingness that every human being eventually undergoes. This is the plunge into nothingness that came about because of the human revolt against God. Jesus Christ's plunge into darkness would have brought about despair and destroyed every other human being. The greater the character of the one who makes this free fall, the greater the annihilation suffered by the individual. No one has undergone death as Christ did because he was life itself. No one was punished for sins as Christ was because he was pure. No one has experienced the crash into the evil nothingness as Jesus did — that terrifying reality that prompted his words, "My God, my God, why have you abandoned me" (Matt. 27:46) — because he was the Son of God. Christ was truly "annihilated." He died while he was still young. His work was stifled before it could flourish. His friends were taken from him. His honor was destroyed. He had nothing left, and he was nothing: "a worm and not a man." In an unthinkable sense, Christ "descended into hell," which is the realm where evil nothingness reigns. He eventually broke the chains of death and evil, but first he endured this realm in a terrifying, incomparable manner.

Christ, the infinitely loved Son of the eternal Father, fell into the depths, to the very ground of evil. He penetrated into that nothingness from which the new creation came, the *re-creatio*. As the ancients said, Christ brought about the second creation of the already existing creation that had not been destroyed into nothingness. He transformed the second creation into a new existence, into the new human community, into the new heaven and the new earth.

Christ hung on the cross. No one can truly comprehend what he went through. Insofar as we become Christian and learn to love the Lord, we begin to sense something: how all action, all struggles ceased on the cross. There was no evasion, no holding back by Christ. Everything — body and heart and spirit — were surrendered in an offering of infinite, total suffering, into a judgment against the guilt of each of us — a judgment that continued without resolution until Jesus' death. . . . At the moment of death Christ reached the depths from which God's all-powerful love called forth the new creation.

If someone were to ask, What is certain? What is so certain that someone can live and die for it? What is so certain that it anchors all else in our lives? — the answer is Christ's love. Life teaches us that what has ultimate significance are not other men and women, not science or philosophy or art or any other human endeavor. Not even the natural world, which is full of deception, nor time, nor destiny. Not even God alone, for sin has stirred up God's wrath. How could we know without Christ what we can expect from God? Only Christ's love is certain. We cannot even say that God's love is certain because we definitely know God's love only through Christ. And if we knew God's love without Christ, we would be troubled because love can be harsh; indeed, as it becomes more noble, it becomes more demanding. We know only through Christ that God loves us with forgiveness. What is certain is what the cross reveals. The conviction that endures, the power that fills our hearts, is that which is often inadequately proclaimed: the heart of Jesus Christ is the beginning and end of all things. And what stands secure — in matters concerning eternal life and eternal death — does so because of Christ. —HE, pt. 5, ch. 14, pp. 485–87

JESUS' RESURRECTION (1937)

The Gospels attest that a mysterious event took place on the third day after Jesus' death. They witness to this event not only in what they say but also in how they say it. They speak of this unique happening in accounts that have sudden interruptions, conflicting testimony, and ambiguities and contradictions that cannot be fully resolved. They show that something extraordinary broke into time and space — something that shattered the usual forms of human experience....

The Gospels convey something extraordinary: Jesus of Nazareth has risen to new life. This is the same Jesus who was the teacher of a small group of disciples, was seen by many people to be the Messiah, and was put to death by his enemies. This Jesus has attained an existence different from that which Socrates spoke about with his disciples before his death. Socrates declared that his soul would experience a better and fuller life — a kind of existence different from the new life of someone who after death conveyed a physical image of himself that impressed itself into the spirit of his followers. Jesus attained a new corporeal existence. After death he awoke to the same life that had been destroyed and broken, but now had assumed a new, transformed condition.

We can feel ourselves protest against this unreasonable claim of Christian faith. If we did not have these feelings, we would have reason to distrust ourselves and to ask whether we've turned the Gospels into fantasies. What the Gospels describe is something extraordinary, something that human reason spontaneously doubts. Not surprisingly, many of Jesus' contemporaries believed the official report that was issued by the authorities declaring that the disciples had come while the guards at the tomb were asleep, and they stole Jesus' body (Matt. 28:11–15).

Jesus' resurrection revealed what from the beginning was the living essence of Jesus, the son of man and the Son of God. When we reflect on our own existence, we can see it as a movement that began in the darkness of childhood, a childhood which we can remember only to some extent. This movement climbs, reaches its summit, and then begins to decline so that it eventually shatters, regardless of whether it is more or less fulfilled or comes to a premature end. This curve of the trajectory of our lives begins at birth and ends at death. After death lies a darkness that is so daunting that it is not clear how we could have even moved into life. The decline of our life's curve ends in a darkness over which hovers a vague sense of hope....

This ordinary movement of human life did not occur in the case of Jesus Christ. The trajectory of life's movement began for him not in birth but arcs backward into eternity. "Before Abraham was, I am" (John 8:58). Some scholars wrongly hold that these words were produced by a mystic of the second century, a hundred-some years after Christ. In fact, these words originated with Jesus. Moreover, the curve of Christ's life does not decline into death but moves throughout his entire life into eternity. "They will kill him, and on the third day he will arise" (Matt. 17:23). The life of Christ has an entirely different depth and breadth, an entirely other relationship to death than ours. In his existence, death is only a transition, though one filled with complex meaning. On the road to Emmaus, Jesus asked his disciples, "Must not the Christ suffer everything in order to go into his glory?" (Luke 24:26). The resurrection brought to full realization what Jesus always bore within himself. To deny the resurrection is to deny everything in Jesus' essence and self-consciousness that is connected with his resurrection. What then remains is not worthy of Christian faith.

The Gospels clearly attest to the visionary experiences of Jesus' followers. The disciples had visions!...This is certain. Yet we must understand what these visions actually entailed. What we automatically think today when we read "it was a vision" is a relatively recent idea of a vision. This modern notion contrasts with the ancient view. This ancient understanding is manifest in the Old Testament where "vision" means "disclosure." It refers not to an experience whose meaning is situated only in the inner life of those to whom Christ appeared. Instead, it involves the coming of a higher, objective reality into human experience. The disciples certainly had visions at Jesus' tomb, on the road to Emmaus, in the upper room, and on the Sea of Galilee. In these events they experienced disclosures of the living Lord. They saw him as a reality that was in the world but did not belong to it. He existed in the parameters of this world but he was the Lord of its laws. To view this reality was greater than and different from seeing a tree at the side of the road or seeing a man as he enters a room. To encounter the risen Christ was a shattering, a breaking apart of all that was familiar. This disruption is reflected in the words of the Gospels: He "appeared." He "disappeared." "All at once" he stood in the room. He arrived and "stood beside them" (Mark 16:9, 14; Luke 24:31, 36). As noted earlier, this singular experience is reflected in the abruptness, interruptions, and contradictions of the biblical accounts. These unique forms of expression were required by the unique content that fractures the usual forms of human speech.

—HE, pt. 6, ch. 1, pp. 489, 491, 496–97

Guardini tried to maintain a balance in his Christological writings by speaking about Christ in relation to the triune God as well as about Jesus Christ in himself.

THE FATHER'S EPIPHANY IN CHRIST (1962)

In the farewell discourse, Jesus says: " 'I am the way, and the truth, and the life. No one comes to the Father except through me. If you know me, you will know my Father also. From now on you do know him and have seen him' " (John 14:6–7).

"Philip said to him, 'Lord, show us the Father, and we will be satisfied.' Jesus said to him, 'Have I been with you all this time, Philip, and you still do not know me? Whoever has seen me has seen the Father. How can you say, "Show us the Father"? Do you not believe that I am in the Father and the Father is in me?' " (John 14:8–10).

Mysterious words! Whoever sees Christ sees the Father. What is meant? One could think that these words are to be understood in an overarching sense as though Jesus had said to his disciples: I was with you, and I have proclaimed the Father to you. So you should know who he is! Jesus has spoken again and again about the Father in parables and in public teaching. We think about the Sermon on the Mount, in which Jesus preached the message of divine providence. In response, we can surrender ourselves to the goodness of the Father; we relinquish the burden of worry and live in confidence. He also said that whoever wishes to be holy should not pose before others in order that they might marvel, but should pray in secret. Then he spoke those beautiful words, "Your Father who sees in secret will reward you" (Matt. 6:6).

Matthew includes Jesus' prayer to the Father in the Sermon on the Mount. In the Lord's Prayer the image of the Father comes powerfully into view. It emerges out of the prayer's words: the image of the king of the heavenly kingdom who bears the hallowed name, gives us our daily bread, forgives us our sins, and delivers us from evil (Matt. 6:9–13).

Whoever is familiar with Holy Scripture soon sees that an overarching, general sense of Jesus and the Father is not conveyed. If Christ had meant to say, "you have learned from my words who the Father is," he would have explicitly said this. But his words run, "Whoever sees me sees the Father." So we must push aside our rationalism, which deals only with ideas. Here it is a matter of seeing a living reality. We must also remember that St. John — in distinction from St. Paul — was a man of the eye, and that in his Gospel the idea of epiphany plays a great role.

"Epiphany" means that something "appears," radiates forth in bodily form. In the Prologue of the Gospel are the words: "we have seen his glory, the glory as of a father's only son, full of grace and truth" (John 1:14). This glory is not only thought, not only sensed, but also seen with one's eyes. Something about the human figure of Jesus became illumined for the apostle John, something that was more than a human reality. The epiphany of the Father — who is concealed in the mystery of God — occurred in the figure of the Lord.

There is an analogy to this epiphany in the human realm. We cannot see someone's soul as such, for it is spirit. However, as soon as we turn to another person in love, we see the beloved's soul in that person's countenance. The lover not only thinks about the beloved's soul, not only arrives at it out of the proper inner experience of the beloved's existence. The lover also sees the soul itself. Indeed one could almost say that in such a moment the beloved's soul is the first thing that the lover sees, and after the soul then the body.

In a similar way, the Gospel says that people who are enlightened by the grace of faith see the Son of God, the eternal Logos, in the physical figure of Jesus of Nazareth. In the First Letter of John the message comes forth with great force. It speaks of "what was from the beginning, what we have heard, what we have seen with our eyes, what we have looked at and touched with our hands concerning the word of life." All senses are awake; however, since they operate in faith, they are capable of more than natural organs on their own. So that the reader does not slip beyond the greatness of the message, the letter states once again, "this life was revealed, and we have seen it and testify to it, and . . . we declare to you what we have seen and heard" (1 John 1:1–3). We feel the insistence. We in faith and with open hearts can encounter Jesus who disclosed in himself the eternal Son.

Now the Lord says, "Whoever sees me sees the Father." What does this mean?

The Son's existence is so vibrant that we must ask, what kind of a father is it who can have such a son? Given the Son's unwavering faithfulness to the Father, what is the vastness of the Father's love?

And still we have not said enough. Jesus did not evince a sonship that led to his own destruction. He is not similar to a son who remains under the oppressive power of an authoritarian father and remains infantile, never coming to maturity. Jesus manifested a wonderful freedom, a powerful peace in himself. He remained faithful because he was entirely individuated in this faithfulness. The Father's command must be respectful of his Son's individuality! What breadth, what nobility! How precious this Father's will must be if Jesus could say that doing his Father's will is his food and drink! The Father must be very close to his Son if such an interior harmony is possible!

Here is a faithfulness, an obedience, that is as great as the command, which itself is great. Fully aware of his Father's presence, Jesus said: "Whatever the Father does, the Son does likewise" (John 5:19).

The conclusion of the Prologue of John's Gospel says, "No one has ever seen God. It is God the only Son, who is close to the Father's heart, who has made him known" (John 1:18). The great intimacy that is conveyed in John's Prologue is expressed again later in the gospel story. The Prologue states: "In the beginning was the Word, and the Word was with God, and the Word was God" (John 1:1). Jesus' nearness to his Father is exhibited again near the end of his life: "Father, into your hands I commend my Spirit" (Luke 23:46). Jesus displayed an interior, filial relationship with his Father, and, as a result, Jesus revealed his Father even when he did not explicitly speak about the Father.

To the degree that Christ becomes clear to us, the Father encounters us. As Jesus said in his farewell discourse, "Whoever has seen me has seen the Father" (John 14:9). Surely this is the stuff not of spiritual psychology but of inner surrender, of prayer. —JB, 52–55, 55–56

THE GOOD SHEPHERD (1963)

Jesus Christ said, "I lay down my life for my sheep" (John 10:15). The covenant of Jesus with those who belong to him lasts through death. It is a union in death. Jesus' gift of himself, which is the Eucharist, flows from Jesus' death. He established this sacrament on the night before his passion. He said, "Take, eat; this is my body." Then, taking the cup, he said, "Drink from it, all of you; for this is the blood of the covenant, which is poured out for many for the forgiveness of sins" (Matt, 26:26–27). Reflecting on the last supper, St. Paul wrote: "For as often as you eat this bread and drink this cup, you proclaim the Lord's death until he comes" (1 Cor. 11:26). The union that Jesus brings about is as deep as that between someone who dies for another person and the person who lives because of another's death. However, in the case of Jesus, the one who does this is almighty God.

However, as in the case of all true relationships, the relationship between Jesus and us also goes in reverse. The image of the journey through the dark valley attains its ultimate meaning because the valley of death is our dying (Ps. 23). There, no one walks beside us — not our father, not our mother, not our brother or sister, neither our loved one nor our friends. There, no assistance comes from science, art, or culture. We go alone through the dark valley. But Christ is there. He alone is there because, after having lived for us, he has died for us, and, rising from the tomb, he has conquered death. In death, he has established a mysterious bond between himself and us. Christ has shared our destiny with such divine power that he lives the life of every believer. As St. Paul has said, "I live, though not I, but Christ lives in me" (Gal. 2:20). Whenever a believer says "I," Christ says "I" in that person. Whenever a believer undergoes death, Christ undergoes it, too.

In a sacred transformation, the Father gives what St. Paul has asked for all believers: "that Christ may dwell in your hearts through faith, as you are being rooted and grounded in love. I pray that you may have the power to comprehend with all the saints, what is the breadth and length and height and depth, and to know the love of Christ that surpasses knowledge, so that you may be filled with all the fullness of God" (Ephesians 3:17–19).

It is possible that we have received a foreshadowing of our death. We may have already sensed the moment when there is absolute isolation, when everything falls aside and withdraws. The greater the influence on our lives of certain words that were previously spoken, the greater the emptiness of what these words promised: wealth, progress, and culture.

Only one specific bond of trust will remain true: trust in Christ. Christ will still be there. He will walk with each of us and will die the death of everyone who believes in him. And Christ will "raise us up on the last day" (John 6:39).

— WP, ch. 9, pp. 205–6

A PRAYER ON JESUS' SELF-EMPTYING (1948)

O Lord, the apostle has said that you were "in the form of God" from all eternity, the Son of the Father, the image of God's holiness, and sharer in God's glory. You did not regard your "divine being" as something stolen, the sort of thing that a thief anxiously seizes. Instead, you generously "emptied" yourself. You took "the form of a slave, being born in human likeness." You came to us in "human form." You "humbled" yourself, and "became obedient to the point of death — even death on a cross" (Phil. 2:7–8).

You came to human beings in their estrangement from God. In your self-emptying, you descended into the depths of our abandonment and have taken us home. Therefore God "highly exalted" you and has given you "the name that is above every name, so that at the name of Jesus every knee should bend, in heaven and on earth and under the earth, and every tongue confess that Jesus Christ is Lord, to the glory of God the Father" (Phil. 2:9–11)

For this reason, O Lord, I bend my knee when your name is spoken and confess that you are the Lord, the redeemer and bearer of salvation.

Sin is blindness. Therefore, I ask you, my redeemer, free me from the deception of pride. Teach me to see who I am and who you are. Move my heart so that I may perceive what you have brought about.

At the time that you, O Lord, reversed our destiny, you were totally alone. You received no understanding and no love from others. Alone you bore our guilt before God's justice. Now you welcome us into your redemption. I ask you, grant that I may know you and be with you with all of my love. Amen.

— TG, ch. 17, pp. 37–38

Chapter 5

Christian Prayer

The voice of the Lord is powerful;
the voice of the Lord is full of majesty.
—Psalm 29:4

Most of us are not good listeners. We hear part of what someone says, but we disregard some of the information, miss what the words imply, and ignore the feelings behind the words. Given our lack of attentiveness, we also do not pray well. Prayer, says Romano Guardini, is a dialogue between God and ourselves. It occurs in private words, meditations, communal devotions, the Mass, and other modes. We speak to God, and God speaks to us. But we do not listen well. Nevertheless, God listens to us — to our complaints and questions as well as to our praise and thanksgiving.

Guardini relied on various types of prayer. He was spiritually nourished by the Mass and the church's liturgy of the hours. At the same time, he needed to pray alone, for example, reciting the Rosary and meditating. Amid this diversity of forms, he perceived the deep human longing for God in response to God's reaching out to us (Rom. 8:23). At the end of his life, Guardini frequently prayed by simply waiting in darkness for God.

PRAYERFUL MOMENTS (1945)

During the recovery from my surgery in 1906, I stayed at Freiburg's university hospital, which was staffed by compassionate nurses. Here I was introduced for the first time to the atmosphere of an abbey. In light of my new inner sense of my calling, this world of tranquility and quiet service made a deep impression on me. Since then I have often come in contact with the world of hospitals, and, although I have had some unpleasant experiences in hospitals, I have always felt a high regard for this world.

I remember well my first visit to the Beuron Abbey. It was evening. We went from the train station directly to the abbey and were welcomed into the cloister itself, since the guest wing was not yet built. Residing in the cloister made our stay warm and life-giving. The rooms were simple, with much brown wood and an indescribable something that made a person feel good in one's depths. Then we received something to eat, and after that we went to evening prayer. The church was already dark, with only a little light in the choir. The monks stood in their places and prayed the beautiful psalms of the evening prayer. A sense of mystery, holy and momentous, dominated the entire church. Later I saw that the liturgy has many powerful and glorious aspects. But evening prayer was the door through which I initially entered into the sacred world of worship. At the start, it was a better entrance for me than the great liturgical ceremonies.

—BML, 78, 87–88

Beginning in the 1600s, the Eucharist was seen as the rite in which the priest "said" the Mass while each member of the congregation watched the priest and quietly prayed the Rosary or other devotions. Contributing to the renewal of the church's worship, Guardini helped recover the ancient understanding of the Mass as the activity of the entire assembly. He distinguished between the liturgy and private prayer, that is, between the formal, structured worship of the believing community and the prayers of individual believers.

WORSHIP AND PRIVATE PRAYER (1918)

The "I" of the liturgy is primarily the whole believing community, a solidarity, the church, which is greater than the sum total of the individuals in the congregation. The liturgy is the church's public official worship. It is led by a priest, a person whom the church specifically selects and commissions for this service. In liturgy, God is worshiped by the spiritual community, which is itself "built up" in and through this worship. It is important to understand the objective character of the liturgy. Here the Catholic notion of communal worship differs from the predominantly Protestant understanding, which highlights the importance of the individual believer. In the Catholic view, because every man and woman is a social being as well as an individual, each believer is spiritually freed and formed by participating in the great unity that is realized in worship.

Along with the highly cultic forms of liturgy, there are forms of devotion that manifest the more personal or individual aspects of prayer. There are, for example, afternoon devotions with hymns, and devotions found only in a specific geographical region, or at a certain time of the year, or for particular occasions. Prayer of this sort bears the flavor of a specific moment or locale and is an immediate expression of the singular creativity of a given community.

Authentic liturgy expresses not the "I" but the "we." This is the case even when an individual believer is required to have a special role (for example, in a personal profession of faith or in specific prayers said by the bishop or the priest). The liturgy is carried out not by individuals but by the community of believers. This community consists not only of the people who are physically present in a church; it is composed not only of the assembled group. It extends beyond the limits of the particular space and encompasses all believers on earth. It also reaches beyond the boundaries of time so that the worshiping community on earth is aware of its unity with those who have died and now abide in eternal life.

It is not appropriate to set up an opposition between the spiritual life of the individual believer with its personal determinations and the life of the liturgy with its set forms for all situations. It is not a matter of either the individual's prayer or the community's worship. There must be both the one and the other in a life-giving interaction.

—VG, ch. 1, p. 17; ch. 2, pp. 32, 46

THE SIGN OF THE CROSS (1929)

When you make the sign of the cross, make it properly. Not a fast, stunted gesture whose meaning is not clear, but a proper sign of the cross, done slowly, grandly, from the forehead to the chest, from one shoulder to the other. Do you sense how it completely encircles you?

Recollect yourself properly. Gather all of your thoughts and your whole heart into this sign, as you go from your forehead to your chest, from shoulder to shoulder. Then you may feel how the sign of the cross completely envelopes you, body and soul. It pulls you together, consecrates you, and sanctifies you.

Why? It is the sign of everything; it is the sign of salvation. On the cross, our Lord redeemed all people, all of history, and the world. Through the cross, Christ sanctifies every human being, entirely, to the last fiber of his or her being.

For this reason, we make the sign of the cross before we pray. It orders and recollects us; it pulls our minds and hearts and wills toward God. After we pray, we again make the sign of the cross so that there remains in us what God has given us. When we are tempted, we make the sign of the cross so that God strengthens us. When we are in danger, we make it so that God safeguards us. When we are given blessings, we make it so that God's abundant life will be received in our souls, and everything in us will be made fruitful and consecrated.

Consider all of this when you make the sign of the cross. It is the sign above all others, the sign of Christ. Make the sign properly: slowly, grandly, thoughtfully. It encircles your whole being, body and soul, your thoughts and your will, senses and heart, your doing and your enduring. In this sign, all will be strengthened, dedicated, consecrated in the power of Christ, in the name of the triune God. —VZ, ch. 1, pp. 13–14

OBSERVATIONS ABOUT PRAYER (1937)

The great things in life unfold in silence. They take place not in the noise and the extravagance of public events but in the clarity of inner seeing, in the quiet movement of reaching a decision, in hidden personal sacrifices and little known accomplishments. They silently occur when one's heart is touched by love, when one's free spirit is called to action, and when a branch bears fruit. The quiet powers are uniquely strong.

—HE, pt.1, ch. 3, p. 12

Jesus brought to earth a sacred reality from the fullness found in God. He released a stream of life into the thirsting world. From "above" he enacted a new kind of existence which could not have come from creation itself and which was built according to a design which from "below" appears to be bewildering and subversive. To participate in this new existence we must open ourselves; we must free ourselves from the entanglements of the natural order of existence and go out to meet that which is coming to us. —HE, pt. 1, ch. 12, p. 80

Illness can prompt personal reflection when the one who is ill does not slip into a dullness and a craving for small pleasures that can accompany sickness. The patient must try to enter into the still space which is situated in the suffering.

—HE, pt. 2, ch. 9, p. 143

At some future time, all that is loud will be silent. All that is visible, publicized, and broadcast will be brought to judgment, and the great transition will commence. At the present, the outer world sees itself as that which is real. The inner world is seen as only added to the outer world as a weak, marginal place in which people can catch their breath when they can no longer remain in the public arena. Eventually though things will be straightened out. What is now silent will then become an evident strength. What is now concealed will then break into the open. Contemplation will be more important than action; being present will have a greater weight than accomplishing something.... Although it is not yet so, a unity will eventually come about; what is within us and what is outside of us will be brought into harmony. —HE, pt. 3, ch. 7, pp. 229–30

We should keep in mind that the kingdom of God is coming. It is no longer tied to a specific historical period, but is now always present and coming to each of us. God's kingdom enters the heart of every man or woman who lets it in. It enters, too, into every community that allows it in, and also into every activity in which it is welcomed. —HE, pt. 2, ch. 10, p. 256

Along with leading in the renewal of the Mass, Guardini contributed to the recovery of ancient forms of private prayer. He urged Christians to learn how to focus or to recollect their hearts and minds so that they can truly listen to God's word.

PRAYER AS PERSONAL RECOLLECTION (1943)

Human beings relate to God in contradictory ways. They yearn for God, sense this yearning, and seek the One who created them and sustains them. Yet they also want nothing to do with God. They evade God and struggle against the Giver of life.

This contradiction shows itself in our relationship to prayer. As we experience and recognize the sacred value of prayer, we sense its truth and feel more drawn to pray. Nevertheless, we avoid prayer. This avoidance has many causes. One of these, as mentioned above, is the ambivalence that we feel toward God. Another is that we do not readily see God in our lives. Or, to be more precise, we do not immediately see God in the things and people around us. We notice these concrete realities and observe how they function or act. We may also be directly affected by them and respond to their pushing and pulling on us so that an interaction occurs between us and them. What we neglect to observe is that God is there too, both revealed and concealed in everything. With eyes of faith, we may see God in the things and people around us. With hearts of love, we may detect God in our lives. But our eyes are often veiled, and our hearts are often insensitive. As a result, we may lack experiences of God.

If we wish to pray well, we must learn how to prepare ourselves for prayer. It can be said in general that prayer is as good as its preparation. What this preparation demands, and how it should be realized, can be approached from various perspectives. Here I shall present prayer as a form of personal recollection.

Recollection requires that we become calm. Usually we are pulled here and there by many things, stimulated by amiable or antagonistic contacts, pressured by demands and fears, by concerns and passions. We are continually interested in attaining something or in keeping away from something, in acquiring or repelling, in doing or undoing. We always want something; we are intent on moving toward a goal or away from a danger.

We must stop our minds from moving from one thing to another. We must focus on what is most important. We must relax and say, "Now I have nothing else to do but to pray. I am reserving the next ten minutes" — or as much time as we set aside — "only for prayer. Everything else must go. I am entirely free only for this." We must be honest with ourselves about how we actually spend these ten minutes. A human being is a sly creature, and the slyness of the human heart shows itself above all in religious matters. As we begin to pray, we will be prompted by our restlessness to do something else. Something else — for example, a project, a conversation, a concern, a responsibility, a newspaper, a book — will suddenly seem very important, and our prayer will stop.

When we reflect on the original meaning of the verb "to recollect," we realize that it means to gather up again, to unite once more. A glance at our lives reveals, however, how little each of us is united, or centered, in ourselves. In order to pray well we must have a secure center within us from which we cope with the various aspects of our lives. We must have a core from which proceeds all activity and to which this activity relates back. From this center, we must differentiate between our most important goals and our less important ones, and from this center, too, we set our priorities among our various activities and experiences. This personal center must be the stable core, the point of continuity amid flux, the essence that unfolds and defines who we are and where we stand in relation to other people. Most of us have not developed a secure center. Today we find this harder to do than the people of earlier generations who lived life more deeply.

This inability to find one's center shows itself in prayer. The spiritual masters often speak about dissipation, about the condition in which our lives have neither a center nor a unity. In this condition, our thoughts stray from one thing to the next, our feelings remain unclear, and our willpower is not strong. When we are dissipated, we are not "someone," and, as a result, we lack the ability to express ourselves and receive responses from others. We possess only a tangle of thoughts, a flow of experiences, and a stream of impressions. Thus personal recollection requires "pulling things together," as the word "recollection" implies. We must direct our attention to that which we want to do, and we must hold in check our wandering thoughts and concerns—a most difficult task! Thus we collect ourselves once again and become united souls who are disposed to pray. As centered selves, we can hear the divine call and respond as Moses did, "Here I am" (Exod. 3:4).

A last comment: to recollect oneself means to wake up. When we are dissipated, we usually have a certain air about us: We are anxious about something. We are restless to get underway toward a goal. We are preoccupied about a project. Then, as soon as we relax, we find ourselves emotionally empty and intellectually dull. When we are no longer pulled toward a specific goal, when no task makes demands on us, when nothing attracts our attention, then we fall apart; we feel a certain vacuum and a dimwittedness. The desolation that we now endure is somehow connected with the restlessness that had shaped our behavior. This is not unlike the fact that people with violent passions are often cold-hearted. In any case, our emptiness and dullness are somehow the underside of our restlessness. By contrast, when we are calm and capable of recollecting ourselves, when we become still and go into our depths, we awaken interiorly. Our calm and inner wakefulness go together; they sustain and influence each other.

As we recollect ourselves, we become calm and present, and we move beyond our inner burdens and worries. We find ourselves lifted up — lighter, freer, and brighter. We also awaken our attentiveness so that we can energetically direct ourselves toward God. We open our inner eyes so that we see more clearly and accurately. In short, we dispose ourselves to an encounter with God.

Personal recollection is not one discrete act among others, but the proper condition or state of our inner lives. It orients us to enter into the right relationships with other persons and things.

Recollection generates an inner openness or receptivity so that in prayer we can say, "Here is God." My description of this experience makes it seem as though things occur in a sequence. This is not the case. In actuality, this form of prayer is a coherent whole, consisting of personal recollection, the opening of sacred space in oneself, an awareness of God's presence, and a sense of standing before God. We can recollect ourselves only because God turns toward us. We can say with sacred meaning, "I am here," only because God, attentive to us, is there and welcomes us. God creates the sacred space by coming to us — the space that we discover through recollection and in which we stand when we are recollected. God determines the sacred space where each of us belongs, where we find ourselves and the world, where we hear God's voice and are able to respond.

In discussing prayer, we must keep this whole together so that our thoughts do not get tangled up.

Recollection disposes us to acknowledge, "Here is God, the living and holy One, of whom divine revelation speaks. And here also am I." This "I" is not, however, the undefined individual of daily life, the preoccupied person who cares for things at home, hurriedly walks down the street, and works throughout the day. Rather this "I" is the one who is responsible for his life. This "I," though existing in spiritual poverty, cannot be someone's possession or property and cannot be controlled by anyone. This "I" is the person whom God intended when God created me, the man or woman to whom the words apply, "God and my soul, otherwise there is nothing in the world." I am the one who exists first of all in relation to God.

—VB, ch. 1, pp. 16–17, 18, 19, 20–22, 24–25

In the aftermath of the Third Reich and the Second World War, Guardini discussed the value of praying the Rosary.

THE ROSARY (1949)

Oppressive events move throughout time and lay a heavy hand on the lives of us all. Questions regarding our own fate and the destiny of those who are close to us arise; above all, the destiny of the human family engages our minds and our hearts. The effect is felt in many ways in religious belief. Some people may discard prayer entirely because they are surfeited or shaken. They must see that they regain their inner balance; they must try to hear and recognize again the quiet voices next to the loud, to sense that God always remains God, no matter how powerful earthly influences may be.... With other people it is the opposite, and the vicissitudes of life remind them of the eternal. They feel that things cannot be carried out in a purely worldly way, but must be laid before God. The more decisive someone is, the more necessary God is. People long for a place of quiet in which they can meditate and gather strength and then later return to their tasks with fresh assurance. They need a prayer that gives them a lingering chance to pause, to collect and strengthen themselves. Such a prayer is the Rosary. It has served many people well. It is about the Rosary that I wish to speak.

We should begin with what is most obvious in the Rosary. An aid is used in this prayer, a string or a chain of beads. Some of these beads are larger than others, or marked apart from others by a greater distance. Ten smaller beads follow a larger one, and they form a "decade." The whole chain has five such decades. They are preceded by a sort of preface, formed by a little crucifix and followed by one large and three smaller beads.

This string of beads slides through the fingers of the person who prays. At the little cross in the beginning, we say the Creed; at every smaller bead, the Hail Mary. At the larger ones, which always precede a row of the ordinary beads, we pray the "Our Father," "the Lord's Prayer." After every decade comes the doxology: "Glory be to the Father, and to the Son, and to the Holy Spirit; as it was in the beginning, is now, and ever shall be, world without end. Amen." And all begins and ends with the sign of the cross.

What does all of this mean? Is not this praying cord a symptom of inferior piety, as the critics say? Is it not something material that contradicts Jesus' word of exhortation: "God is spirit, and they who worship God must worship in spirit and in truth" (John 4:24)?

The Rosary belongs to a form of prayer that is centered around a sojourn with God, around a service to God — in inner self-knowledge and tranquility, but in a manner that makes a flowing channel out of the words in which it is expressed, a force that keeps it moving. In this case, new words will not always emerge, but the same words will return. Repetition becomes the outer form of prayer with the purpose of pacifying and fulfilling the inner emotion. The litany is such a prayer, with its many related invocations and petitions in which the thought is slowly transformed. It is very old; we find it at the dawn of Christendom. A similar kind of prayer is the use of the psalms, when the "antiphon" is inserted between the verses — a constantly recurring invocation. The antiphon, too, is as old as the hills. Belonging to this form of prayer as repetition is also the Rosary.

The Rosary represents a certain type of religious devotion. Individual persons may claim that they cannot do anything with it. That is their business. But they must not call this prayer senseless or unchristian because then they will show their ignorance.

The string of beads obviously has the purpose of diverting the thoughts from certain external distractions. One bead leads the person-at-prayer to the next bead. The ten beads in a decade keeps the repetition within certain bounds, approved by long usage. Otherwise the person at prayer would have to keep watch for the "too little" or else fall into the "too much," and thus be diverted from the essential. The beads take this trouble off the person's shoulders. They do the counting for us. Yet is this not something "technical"? Surely; but does not all of life contain "technicalities"? It is said of all things, even the spiritual, that they have to be learned. But learning requires practice; and practice is nothing else but a training of technical skill, liberating our strength and attention for what is essential. So long as I am yet "unskilled," I must watch every single act, and the essential comes off badly. But with the acquisition and development of technical skill, the essential is liberated. The string of beads has no other meaning.

The Rosary consists of holy words. The "Hail Mary" takes precedence over all. Its first part is derived from the New Testament. It begins with the message of the angel in Nazareth. "Hail, full of grace, the Lord is with you." This is followed by the words with which Elizabeth greeted Mary when she crossed the mountains to visit her: "Blessed are you among women, and blessed is the fruit of your womb" (Luke 1:28, 42). The second part is an ancient appeal for Mary's intercession.... Christ himself gave us the "Our Father" as the perfect model and substance of all Christian prayer.... The Creed forms the first expression of Christian conviction.... The "Glory be to the Father and to the Son and to the Holy Spirit" is the glorification of the triune God in its simplest form.... Finally, in making the sign of the cross, with which the Rosary begins and ends — "In the Name of the Father and of the Son and of the Holy Spirit" — Christians since antiquity have placed themselves under the name of God and the sign of redemption.

The words of the prayers recur. They create that open, moving world, transfused by energy and regulated by reason, in which the act of prayer takes place. As soon as the person-at-prayer utters the words, he or she has built a home of speech. The history of the person's own language and life becomes animated. Behind it is the history of the person's people, interwoven into that of humanity. When the words are those of Holy Scripture, they become an arch of the sacred room of revelation where the truth of the living God is made known to us.

— RLF, ch. 1, pp. 7–22

During his last years, Guardini reflected further on the experience of prayer as a dialogue between God and ourselves. These reflections were published after his death.

SPEAKING WITH GOD (1976)

To pray means to speak with God. This action presupposes that God wishes to speak with us. We cannot pray in a vacuum. God must be there, and must be a "someone," a "you," not a mere "it." Further, prayer cannot occur on the basis of our own initiative. God must make it possible. God summons it, sustains it, and draws it forth. Prayer is a response to "someone" who makes it possible. One may ask, how is prayer experienced? Prayer can proceed even in dimness, in apparent emptiness; it can persist because of a conviction that is inexplicable. At such a time, prayer moves toward what Blaise Pascal called an "infinitely fine point." The "emptiness" in which prayer can occur at times is not, however, nothingness. Rather this emptiness is equivalent to a "fullness." The dimness is not darkness but the equivalent of light. As prayer takes place, these equivalents become evident. The life of prayer is realized in the form of a conversation. It is possible because God is the One who revealed himself in the burning bush at Mount Horeb (Exod. 3)....

In truth, the center of human existence stands in relation to God's revelation. It is not that human beings exist as wholly autonomous individuals, who secondarily may seek a relationship with God if they are disposed to do so, or if they feel the need to do so. On the contrary, a relationship with God is essential to existing as a human being. We are incomplete as human beings when we do not enter into this fundamental relationship with God. In this relationship — which permeates all aspects of human life and all that occurs in our lives — we become aware of the fact that we are unavoidably related to God at the very center of our being, even when we deny God or neglect God. In this relationship with God, each of us discovers his or her own autonomy and receives the power to become more individuated.

Indeed, we gain self-confidence and the strength to resist the impersonal forces that operate in our time. —EC, 44–45

A PRAYER ON PRAYER (1948)

Lord and God, you are the Giver of life, the One who dwells in and guides all of creation. All things are images of your glory, and all events attest to your activity among us. But our seeing is impaired. We do not perceive the deeper reality of things. Also, our ears do not hear your voice. You are the one true reality; you are present in all your works. Wherever we are, we are before you. But our hearts are dull and only occasionally notice your sacred presence.

So, it is often wearisome, O Lord, to remain in prayer before you. We often look into the darkness and find no place where we can rest. We often speak into the silence and hear no answer. When we free ourselves from the demands of the things around us and try to come before you, we frequently find ourselves in a vacuum. Then our efforts seem pointless to us, and this experience prompts us to return to what's familiar to us.

Lord, teach us not to trust these disheartening experiences of prayer. Prayer should not be an expression of our needs. Instead, it is the sacred service that we owe to your honor and that we need to do for the good of our souls.

So I ask that you teach me to do this service of prayer with faithfulness. I want to come beside you and remain there, even when I think that I am alone. I want to speak to you and believe that my words reach your heart, even when you do not appear to answer.

I want to bear the burden of prayer as long as this pleases you—but let the silence not last for too long. Let me sense that I am with you. Your divine revelation speaks of your countenance shining over us. Show me, Lord, your sacred face so that

I may know the One to whom I am speaking. I believe that you love me. Let me enter into your heart and be embraced by your love. Amen. —TG, ch. 23, pp. 49–50

Two years before his death, Guardini sensed that he was nearing the end of his life. Feeling weak and vulnerable, he moved toward a deeper trust in God — a trust that even included a sense that God had abandoned him.

A LETTER ON TRUST IN GOD (1966)

My dear friend, I would like to pass on to you some ideas that are the fruit of my long illness. I have reflected — not superficially but in some depth and accuracy, I believe — on the condition of our human existence. The stimulus for these thoughts was the continuing experience of illness and pain and, as a result of these, the question whether it is possible to fashion something meaningful out of our human existence.

I saw first of all that there are not merely illness and pain, but that the illness and the pain are always connected with movement into life. Simultaneously I realized that when we adversely affect another person, we suffer with the other person. This insight seems valid for everything in life. When there is the rare case of someone being always healthy and always mentally alert, then some kind of spiritual illness emerges out of this favorable condition — a spiritual illness about which one could also speak. These reflections generate yet another insight. Both pessimism, which says that everything is bad and depressing, and optimism, which says that everything is good and uplifting, are false. Our human existence is a tangled mix of both. Both pessimism and optimism are contained in every moment of life.

What is someone to do then? I have looked for one word that could express the correct stance that we should take toward life, and I have found it: trust.

Trust in what? In life? Trust in the order of personal existence? It would be inadequate to trust in an abstraction. There must be something more. Our trust must be in the One who has created the world, who sustains it, and who ultimately governs it. The decisive element is God's gracious intention that wills God's life with us. It is God's wisdom, which is manifest in the weaving of our existence and which also sees that this weaving is at times tangled because since the beginning of time something destructive has been at work in creation, namely, the revolt against God and God's intention for creation. This decisive element is finally a power, which will ultimately bring about the victory of God's intention for the well-being of our lives.

Thus trust in God is the primary thread for being able to make one's way through life.

To make this act of trust in God took much thought and, beyond that, a shaping of my will. Trust in its full sense involves embodying the correct way of relating to others. If you think it through, you will see that only this thread runs completely through life's complexities and mix-ups. To have recognized the importance of trust was the fruit of reflecting on the unfolding of my life, that is, of my search for the truth during a long period of illness.

Each of my sentences here invites more sentences concerning definitions, other complexities, and further clarifications. But I have refrained from trying to prove anything, from attempting to lead you through the experience itself to the validity of my thought about it. I have pushed myself to come to one encompassing insight from the things that I thought about over many days and nights of illness. I do not want to move you to some kind of optimism. Everything that is difficult and hard was contained in my experience. I sought to find something which makes sense of and responds to all that occurred. To have found the important thread in this word "trust" is to have found a way to deal with all that illness entails.

Someone could ask, is the effort to bring together and arrange every aspect of our lives simply part of the confusion? The answer is a decisive no. Our search for meaning is right. All that exists — with the exception of God — is essentially connected with the tapestry of life. God alone, the One who simply is, exists out of God's self and in God's self and requires no preconditions. So, for us, God is pure mystery. We cannot comprehend God. We can only think about the words that God speaks to us, that is, about divine revelation.

I ask that you think about what I have said. It seems that the way to trust God is for each of us to trust another person, and in this way everyone will eventually attain the proper trust in God. That you may succeed in coming to trust in God is my wish for you. —TBF, 62–64

A PRAYER DURING A TIME OF SUFFERING (1965)

Living God,
  we believe in you.
Teach us to understand this hour,
  in which it is
  as though you have abandoned us,
    you whose faithfulness is eternal,
  as though you are not the One who told us your name:
    the One who is present to us.
Living God, we believe in you.
Give us the strength to persevere
  when everything becomes meaningless.

Almighty Father,
you who live, Lord, in yourself, needing nothing,
Eternally free, you have created the world,
although you do not need it.
The world exists because you desire that it exists,
filled with your thought.
No earthly sense can discern the intention
from which the world originated.
However, the Revealer, the Son,
has given us the word that means love.
Your love, Father, springs from no earthly heart.

We believe in you,
for what the world means to us are your divine works.
You have conceived them,
You have willed that they should exist, and that
they should continue and shine through you alone.
You direct everything, even our small lives.
You direct our lives
through the soundless guidance of your mystery.
We trust in your love alone.
Nevertheless your magnanimity requires ours.
You have given the world into our hands,
You desire that we should think your thoughts and
work for your ordering of things.

Christ Jesus,
Redeemer of the world,
who returned to the Father
once everything was accomplished.
You are seated at God's right hand on the throne of glory,
awaiting the hour
in which you will come again in power,
to judge the living and the dead.
We believe in you.

Teach us to live out the solitary faith that
this hour demands of us,
this hour when your light appears not to shine,
and yet sheds light even more powerfully
in the darkness than ever before.
In your mystery of life, in your obedience, in greatness
you were obedient to the Father,
saving everything and everybody.
Let your love for us not be in vain.

Most Holy Spirit,
sent to us,
staying with us even when our space sounds empty
as though you were far away.
The ages are given into your hands.
In the mystery of silence you guide
and bring everything to fulfillment.
Therefore we believe and await the coming world.
Teach us to wait in hope.
Allow us to participate in the coming world,
so that the promise of glory will be realized in us.

—TBF, 65–66

MODERN SPIRITUAL MASTERS SERIES

Other volumes in this series are available at your local bookstore or directly through Orbis Books.

Karl Rahner

Spiritual Writings

Edited with an Introduction
by Philip Endean

ISBN 1-57075-533-1

Edith Stein

Essential Writings

Selected with an Introduction
by John Sullivan, OCD

ISBN 1-57075-428-4

Alfred Delp, SJ

Prison Writings

Introduction by Thomas Merton

ISBN 1-57075-524-8

Pedro Arrupe

Essential Writings

Selected with an Introduction by Kevin Burke
Foreword by Peter-Hans Kolvenbach

ISBN 1-57075-549-9